WRITING LIVES
is the DEVIL!

By the Same Author

This Wild Abyss
The Story of the Men Who Made Modern Astronomy

In the Presence of the Creator
Isaac Newton and His Times

Fox at the Wood's Edge
A Biography of Loren Eiseley

WRITING LIVES
is the DEVIL!

Essays of a Biographer at Work

GALE E. CHRISTIANSON

Archon Books
1993

First published 1993 as an Archon Book, an imprint of
The Shoe String Press, Inc.
Hamden, Connecticut 06514.
Printed in the United States of America.

The paper used in this publication meets the minimum requirements of
American National Standard for Information Sciences—Permanence of
Paper for Printed Library Materials. ANSI Z39.48-1984 ⊗

Library of Congress Cataloging-in-Publication Data

Christianson, Gale E.
Writing lives is the devil : essays of a biographer at work
Gale E. Christianson
p.   cm.
Includes bibliographical references and index.
1. Biography as a literary form.   I. Title.
CT21.C48 1993   93—22847   808′06692—dc20
ISBN 0-208-02382-8

Portions of this work have appeared in an earlier form as follows:
"Writing Lives is the Devil!" in *North Dakota Quarterly*; "The Biographer and
the Widow" under the title "Widow's Pique" in *Philadelphia Magazine*;
parts of " 'Old RU' and 'The Gaff' " as "Loren Eiseley in Lincoln: Two
Poems and a Remembrance" in *Prairie Schooner*.

To the memory of my grandparents

Antone and Anna Christianson
Jess and Jesse Lester

Life can only be understood backwards; but it must be lived forwards.

KIERKEGAARD

Contents

Preface

Having recently completed my third volume of biography, I experienced, as before, a wrenching post-partum depression. My brain child, with whom I had carried on a sustained and intimate dialogue during the course of a long gestation, was suddenly mine no longer. My thoughts turned to Edward Gibbon and the night of June 27, 1787, when, in his Swiss summerhouse between the hours of eleven and twelve, he wrote the last lines of the last page of *The Decline and Fall*:

> After laying down my pen, I took several turns in a covered walk of acacias, which commands a prospect of the country, the lake and the mountains. The air was temperate, the sky was serene, the silver orb of the moon was reflected from the waters, and all nature was silent. I will not dissemble the first emotion of joy on the recovery of my freedom, and, perhaps, the establishment of my fame. But my pride soon humbled, and a sober melancholy was spread over my mind, by the idea that I had taken an everlasting leave of an old agreeable companion, and that whatever might be the future fate of my *History*, the life of the historian must be short and precarious.

As the daily pain of confronting the blank page fades, it is replaced by a nostalgia for the worlds the biographer has lost—in my case the Restoration England of Isaac Newton, the largely forgotten Nebraska of Loren Eiseley's youth, the stone and mortar structures from which Copernicus and Galileo gazed upon the stars, the one with his unaided eyes, the other with

a magnifying glass of magical properties the Domini-
cans branded the "Devil's sceptre."

And such is the price of literary craftsmanship that
the reader of biography, like the avid movie-goer, sees
nothing of the material left on the cutting room floor.
Neither is the reader a party to the creative struggle
itself, to the gathering of the mounds of information, to
the sifting and winnowing, to the writing and the rewrit-
ing, to the small triumphs and the nagging doubts when
commitment fails to imitate art, as seems inevitable.

Although these thirteen essays (a baker's dozen we
used to call them when I was growing up in rural Iowa)
were written in a little over a year, they are the annals
of a long and uncompleted journey. Moreover, they are
all of a piece. I set them down in midcareer, between
longer works, lest the opportunity for such reflection
pass me by, for as Gibbon notes, "the life of the historian
must be short and precarious."

As indicated by the subtitle, these pieces constitute
the personal reflections of a biographer at work, nothing more, and, I hope, nothing less. They set forth no
rules or regulations, no axioms or diktats, no paradigms
or universal principles. Nor is this a "how-to guide"
filled with salient wisdom for the benefit of aspiring
biographers, with the author posing as self-deprecating
model. And while the essays herein have benefitted
greatly from the reading I have undertaken on the
subject, they are not a compendium of what my fellow
academics, biographers, and reviewers have previously
written. Finally, although the work draws heavily from
personal experience, it is not autobiography in the
accepted sense of the word.

I have tried to capture a certain intimacy in these
pages, as if the reader were peering over my shoulder.
To facilitate this process, the essays, though somewhat
loosely arranged, speak to the problems and issues

faced by the biographer in more or less chronological order. Thus, "A Conversation with Copernicus" addresses the first and most fundamental of questions: Why does one choose to write the life of X rather than Y, to bond oneself to another human being in a union more symbiotic than matrimony? Once this decision is made, what happens when the life of that person enters totally into one's own?

Two essays on the great Newton follow, but fear not; there are no equations to interrupt the prose. Things of a less substantial nature tip the balance—a lock of silver hair three centuries old, some chemical traces of lead and mercury, letters, both vanished and preserved, broken promises, a loss of faith. Such is the meager evidence with which the biographer must piece together the cause for one of history's most enigmatic mental breakdowns, and the demise of an ill-fated romance.

It has been said of more than one uncooperative survivor, Georglie Yeats and Holly Stevens among them, that she should be shot. Doubtless the sentiment is unjust, but for a time, I entertained vaguely similar thoughts of Mabel Eiseley, who guarded the memory and certain papers of her husband's with a passion put to use. Only after long months of temporizing and numerous false starts was I at last granted an audience with the grandame. What happened both during and after that fateful encounter is chronicled in "The Biographer and the Widow," a story of history on a limited and highly personal scale. So, too, "The Lady of the Masque," wherein lost love and a forgotten tragedy are resurrected through a combination of luck and a year's hard detective work.

How easy it is to forget that history was once the special province of wise elders of the tribe, of bards and wandering minstrels, of soothsayers and epic poets, of unlettered men whose tongues and gestures were the pen and paper of their time. Such are "Old RU" and "The Gaff," keepers of the oral tradition in this dying century. As youths sixty years ago, they walked the streets and countryside surrounding Lincoln, Nebraska, with Eiseley, reciting Tennyson by heart, as it was recited into my tape recorder during my biographical quest, reconstructing a delicate but enduring web of memory.

Yet it is the archives to which the biographer most commonly repairs, passing much of his time in what has been described as dull and unrewarding work. Still, it is here, by piecing together seemingly disparate and obscure connections, that the accomplished writer of a life gets to know his subject better than he knew himself. And on occasion there surfaces some overlooked or well-hidden gem that flings the biographer back to a point where history and his own life collided, producing "A Shiver in the Archives."

The subsequent essay, which begins with the death of my grandfather when I was seven, deals with more subtle "Tools of the Trade": the influence of childhood memories and juvenile literature, the important figures of one's youth, the use of a pencil in the absence of a typewriter, the onset of the computer age and the sacrifice of habit, the reading of fine writing while attempting to approximate it oneself.

Be not deceived! Following the research comes the truly difficult part. Writing lives is exactly what the title of this volume, drawn from a quote by Virginia Woolf, says it is, else the novelist might have employed her talent to compass the lives of real people. Like the writer of fiction, the biographer must face that moment of abject terror when the red light flashes on and the literary oil ceases to flow. While stuck in the middle of Newton's life, I harbored thoughts of entering into a bargain with "the great, dark, bearded one" of Dante's recurring dream, the theme of "Writing Lives Is the Devil!"

"Arrows in the Blue" covers rather different emotional terrain. The titling of books and chapters is one of my great passions, acquired from a lifetime of reading Jack London, Mark Twain, Charles Dickens, Arthur Koestler, and other masters of the game. "Titular obsession," a reviewer for *The New York Times* called it, a mania that afflicted such literary lights as Hemingway, who is said to have had another thirty titles in reserve should Max Perkins, his editor at Scribner's, veto "For Whom the Bell Tolls." Unlike my previous editors, Perkins chose not to exercise his veto, informing the mercurial novelist of his belief that "the writer should always be the final judge," to which I say, Amen!

Historians are trained not to engage their subjects on a first name basis, nor are they permitted to employ the first person "I," what Gibbon once denounced as "the most disgusting of pronouns." To do so is supposedly to shatter the illusion of objectivity, the boundary of good taste demanding distance between the author and reader. Yet how liberating it has been, while composing this group of essays, to invoke both the first person and first names, as I have never been free to do before. I confess that I owe it all to that nefarious trio of my youth, "Tom, Dick, and Harry," whom the reader doubtless knows as well as I.

Melancholy, like darkness visible, descends once more. Driving across the plains of central Illinois in the dead of winter, the biographer reflects on his latest brain child, soon to be released into an equally harsh and unforgiving landscape. How he wishes that, for the moment at least, he were anything but the writer who must endure the equivalent of the Chinese water torture, otherwise known as the drip, drip, drip of reviews. In a rite of self-flagellation, he recounts the long and tortuous struggle that is behind him now. But the times are not yet fulfilled, and what awaits is anyone's guess— almost certainly not Nirvana and hopefully no "Rendez- vous in Hell," one aggrieved author's promise of revenge to an unkind critic.

Finally, if history repeats itself, the first of several dozen fan letters will begin to arrive about the time the first review sees the light of day. These sometimes demeaning, occasionally elevating, frequently comic, but never dull offerings are chronicled in "Comes the Postman," the dozen-plus-one offering added to safe- guard against the possibility that the first twelve might weigh light, thus depriving the reader of his due.

1

A Conversation with Copernicus

In all the times we had eaten lunch together, the distinguished scholar seated across the table from me had never once cracked a joke. He was, I had come to believe, one of those rare individuals who possesses no sense of humor. Then came the day when he launched into a story that actually seemed headed for a punch line. Indeed, I was already smiling in anticipation. It involved the subject of his recently completed biography, a magnum opus referred to as "a five pound wristbuster" by one uncharitable reviewer, who had literally weighed it on his bathroom scale.

Why, when one considers the many great figures in history, my fellow biographer kept asking himself, had he chosen to write the life of X instead of Y, chosen to bond himself to a specific individual in a union more symbiotic than matrimony? Unable to resolve this question after years of introspection, he had finally turned to a psychoanalyst for help.

By this time I was leaning across the table, sandwich poised in midair. Never could I have conceived of this hard-bitten pillar of the academic community asking anyone for assistance in sorting out his deepest motives, much less a disciple of the unconscious. So what if the joke was generic; it must be damned funny if he had

1

taken the trouble to memorize and shape it to his own purpose.

The pitch of his voice did not vary a note as he delivered the ending: "The sessions were well worth it; I finally feel as though I have a true understanding of my identification with . . ." You should consider trying it yourself."

The expression on my face must have been one of incredulity, for my normally staid friend winced. Equally embarrassed myself, I lacked the nerve to ask what he had found so illuminating about the experience. And since he volunteered nothing more on the subject, I remain in the dark to this day.

Whatever one's attitude regarding psychoanalysis, there is little question that its practice has exercised a powerful influence on biographers of all stripes. Whether or not they employ the nomenclature, few research and write as they would have prior to Freud. Paramount in this regard is the question of motives, which are dissected and scrutinized as never before. The coming to grips with idiosyncrasies and seeming contradictions of character displayed by their subjects is now an accepted, indeed obligatory, part of the biographical process.

Equally influential are Freud's insights into early childhood. Biographers were quick to realize that if one would understand the adult one must understand his oldest memories and earliest experiences—that the child is indeed mother and father of us all.

Among more important aspects of the training of psychiatrists is the requirement that they themselves undergo intensive analysis. Because they must relive all the experiences, both disastrous and triumphant, of their patients, it is deemed crucial that they have a detailed guide to their own psychological terrain. Otherwise, the danger is great that the process of identification will turn inward, causing the analyst to focus on the details of his own psychic biography rather than on those of the person seeking his counsel.

One could, I suppose, make a similar case for the training of the biographer, who, after all, is closer to his subject than the analyst to his patient, if only because he deals with but one at a time—a very long time. Many are those who have set out to write a life, then discovered that what they are composing is a thinly veiled autobiography. As in psychoanalysis, problems of judgment often depend on self-knowledge.

Yet the wisdom of philosophers aside, does not the biographer run some considerable risk of becoming too self-searching for his own good? "The despairs and defeated ambitions of former men and women tend to become the despairs and doubts of our own lives," wrote biographer Robert Gittings. "They even make us doubt what we are doing in their exploration. To some, one can imagine, biography could become a self-defeating art. Truth can be lethal. Human life thrives on healthy illusion."[1]

Walking home alone after our unsettling luncheon, I remember thinking that if my friend truly had to know why he had chosen to live for two decades with a person from another century, he was better off finding out after the fact. Still, the wheels continued to turn. Why had I committed five years of my own life to an intractable genius named Isaac Newton, then, skipping two centuries, given another five years to Loren Eiseley, the melancholy essayist of the middle border?

Taking the part of the analyst and employing Freud's technique of abreaction, that is, leading the patient back in roughly chronological order to the moment of truth, I envisioned myself in a high school classroom during my sophomore year. Perspiring heavily, I am bent over a textbook, vainly attempting to solve a problem. A burly young man in need of a shave stands over my shoulder, arms folded, shaking his head in disdain. The youth, who a few months earlier had breezed through Algebra I and II, is floundering on Euclid, harried by a martinet who believes the classroom is an extension of the football field whose sidelines he paces every Saturday night, screaming at his players over broken plays, jumping up and down when an opponent fails to rise after a crunching tackle. I, who weigh no more than 150 pounds fully clothed, vow revenge and get it some twenty-six years later on the publication of a biography of Isaac Newton, the formulator of the calculus and greatest mathematician of his time.

It is a perfect summer's day in the early 1970s. Having grown to manhood, I have completed my doctorate and am teaching at a university in the Midwest. I have long heard good things about the literary naturalist Loren Eiseley, one of whose slender volumes I have finally gotten around to purchasing at the local mall. I place a lawn chair under the large birch tree in the back yard, hoping to read undisturbed for an hour or two. Afternoon yields to twilight, but I do not heed the call to dinner. The evening star is blinking low on the horizon when I finish the last page, the first time in years I have read an entire book at one sitting. Not only is my mind tingling, I feel the vibrations all the way down to my fingertips; my eyes are misty with tears. Although I have published very little, I swear by Venus that I will one day seek out the prose poet and write his life. Fate will prove me only half as good as my word, for we will never meet.

In psychoanalyzing myself I have saved a tidy sum, but am I right? Another score of unspoken connections between biographer and subject come to mind, but these too may only be postulates masquerading as axioms. Moreover, it was Freud himself who said that no person can plumb his own unconscious without the assistance of a mental detective. But would a trained analyst have led me any closer to the truth?

Perhaps the reasons why one chooses to write a particular life are less important than what happens after that person enters totally into one's own. My initial experience with this unsettling phenomenon came as I was completing an essay on the astronomer Nicolas Copernicus, the first sustained biographical work of my career. There is no satisfactory biography of the man for the simple reason that the details of Copernicus's life are little known, which made me even less prepared for our vivid encounter one winter's afternoon.

Immortal as the architect of the modern solar system (the equivalent of the universe in sixteenth-century Europe), Copernicus placed the sun near the center of the orbiting planets, thus standing the geocentric cosmos of Aristotle and Ptolemy on its head. Copernicus's proof of his theory, for it was only that until the formulation of mathematical laws by Kepler and Newton, was slim indeed, constituting little more than an aesthetic hunch. In addition to the fact that heliocentrism violated the senses—everyone felt the Earth at rest beneath their feet and saw the planets and stars circling the place on which they stood—it defied reason by shattering the comforting boundaries of medieval space.

To contemporary critics of the astronomer it was only logical to suppose that if the Earth did indeed orbit the sun, the arrangement and brightness of the stars ought to undergo constant change. As a constellation is approached from Earth its stars should appear larger, brighter, and farther apart. Conversely, as the Earth moves away from the constellation, toward the opposite side of the sun, these same stars should grow dimmer and appear to move closer together. But such a displacement, termed stellar parallax, was not visible to the naked eye. Either Copernicus was wrong or, unbelievably, the stars are so far distant that Earth's orbit is as nothing compared to the immensity of intervening space.

While ruminating on this large slice of cosmology, it suddenly struck me that Copernicus might have carried the argument further in his mind—that he actually entertained the idea of an infinite universe. Such a view would, I realized, be greeted with skepticism, if not derision, by other historians of science, who had long embraced the position taken by the distinguished Alexandre Koyré: "[I]t was enough for one man to move the earth and to enlarge the world as to make it immeasurable—*immensum*; to ask him to make it infinite is obviously asking too much."[2] Still, the question remained: "Did Copernicus give serious consideration to the concept of infinity?"

Passionately caught up in the question, I plumbed *De revolutionibus* for clues to the astronomer's thinking. One passage in particular gave me reason to hope: "Why therefore should we hesitate any longer to grant it [Earth] the movement which accords naturally with its form, rather than put the whole in commotion—the world whose limits we do not know and cannot know?"[3] Copernicus, it seemed to me, was in favor of keeping an open mind on the question.

Clearly, there was no definitive answer to my quest, although I would like to think I received one late on a December afternoon. I had been wrestling with the question for days and was deeply immersed in writing, when I happened to glance up from my desk. Seated in the reading chair by my study window was a thin, somewhat angular man whose uncut hair lay thick upon his narrow shoulders. He was dressed in a long robe fashioned from dark fur, trimmed at the neck and cuffs with ermine. I recognized him immediately as the canon of Frauenburg Cathedral, a Gothic structure which centuries past stood on the outskirts of Christendom, overlooking a stormy Baltic Sea. From its surrounding ramparts Copernicus made his observations of the northern skies, emerging at dusk and disappearing before dawn into one of the fortified towers he called home.

Our conversation, as in many dreams, was brief and mostly one-sided. I struggled mightily to comprehend the medieval Latin spoken by my guest, a problem compounded by his heavy accent. As best I could tell, Copernicus had often discussed the question of infinity with his older friend and confidant Tiedemann Giese, a fellow canon who had exhorted him to publish his work years earlier than he had. Although fascinated by the idea, Copernicus knew he could never resolve the question to his own satisfaction. Thus, as he wrote in *De revolutionibus*, the dispute "as to whether the world is finite or infinite" is best left "to the philosophers of nature."[4] Besides, his astronomical theory was sufficiently controversial without adding more fuel to the intellectual fires. There was always the danger that some mystic or visionary, like the soon-to-be-condemned monk Giordano Bruno, would embrace the concept, pitting the search for scientific truth against religious authority.

Comforting as it was at the time, for I would have testified in a court of law that Copernicus was actually *there*, I look back on this daydream for what it was—a warning not to be so naive and literal-minded in the pursuit of my subject. A biographer without imagination is doomed to failure, but neither is it any good pretending. "Somehow," as biographer Richard Holmes observed, "you [have] to produce the living effect, while remaining true to the dead fact. The adult distance—

the critical distance, the historical distance—[has] to be maintained."[5] More simply put, the biographer must identify but never fuse with his subject.

This is obviously easier said than done. Walking an emotional tightrope, Stephen B. Oates, author of a powerful biography of Martin Luther King, Jr., tells the story of how King's teachings affected him personally. "I suffered a devastating tragedy in my life while I was writing his, and I almost succumbed to a paralyzing bitterness. But I learned from his example how to love again and 'keep on keepin' on' despite my shattered dreams. In a strange and miraculous way the very man I re-created became a warm, sympathetic friend." Oates spoke to the civil rights leader in his dreams, and even found himself imitating King's speech pattern when on the lecture circuit. Then came the replay of that fateful evening in Memphis: "I was stricken with an overwhelming sense of loss, as though a member of my family had been killed. After I sent him home to Atlanta, to be buried near his Grandmother Williams, whom he had loved so as a boy, I left my typewriter and staggered into my living room filled with grief, unable to believe or to bear what had happened. And I cried."[6]

Oates unabashedly employs the word "love," whose presence is palpable in this wrenching anecdote. Richard Holmes, biographer of the romantic poets Shelley and Keats, writes that "If you are not in love with [your subjects] you will not follow them—not very far, anyway." But Holmes further observes that this emotion must be treated as "pre-biographic." The biographic process itself begins "precisely at the moment, at the places, where this naive form of love and identification breaks down."[7]

Such a moment occurred while Holmes was faithfully retracing Robert Louis Stevenson's twelve-day journey through the Cevennes mountains of central France, which Stevenson had recounted ninety years before in *Travels With A Donkey*. A certain tension built with the passing days, Holmes recalls, the feeling that Stevenson was waiting for his fellow Englishman, in person, somewhere up the trail. Then came the evening when Holmes, leading his own recalcitrant donkey, crossed the bridge over the Allier into Langogne. As shadows claimed the streets, the sense of an imminent encounter became overpowering. Holmes returned to the bridge and began pacing up and down, waiting for a sign. "And then I saw it, quite clearly against the western sky, the old bridge of Langogne. It was about fifty yards downstream, and it was broken, crumbling, and covered with ivy. So Stevenson had crossed *there*, not on this modern bridge. There was no way of following him, no way of meeting him. His bridge was down. It was beyond my reach over time, and this was the true sad sign." The revelation plunged Holmes into the blackest gloom. "It was stupid, but I was almost tearful." After eating supper he climbed a steep hill covered with rustling trees and set forth on the path to St. Flour, for he could no longer bear to remain in Langogne.[8]

In that single instant the biographer went from hero-worshipper to partner and friend. When it came time to write of his pursuit of Stevenson, Holmes entered into a mental dialogue with his subject as they moved over the same historical ground, the same trail of events. Together they reviewed the questions of motive and consequence, a steady if subliminal exchange of judgments, attitudes, and conclusions. Holmes's moment of personal disillusion was also the moment of impersonal, objective rebirth.

It would be interesting to know whether this process works in reverse. Apparently the only person capable of loving the young Adolf Hitler was his mother, which says much about the man he would become. It seems inconceivable that any sane biographer could approach such a figure without a strong feeling of contempt, if not outright hatred. The very thought of spending years immersed in the human cesspool that became the Third Reich makes one shudder. How does the biographer enter into a rational dialogue with a madman? The answer, of course, is that he doesn't, but somehow he must come to think of his subject as if he can.

Even more than the figures we admire, the case of a Hitler, a Savonarola, or a Nero raises one of the most serious questions facing the biographer. Holmes notes that writing a life constitutes an act of psychological trespass, "an invasion of the present upon the past, and in some sense the past upon the present."[9] Weighing the thoughts and deeds of other human beings out of the context of their times is both dangerous and unfair. By the same token, when motives and actions are regarded primarily within their historical setting, critical evaluation is at a discount, rendering history useless as a moral as well as an intellectual pursuit.

As both teacher and biographer, I have found myself impaled on the horns of this dilemma more times than I can remember, but never more vividly than when I was writing Newton's story as master of the Mint. Having successfully managed the great recoinage of the late 1690s, Newton could not savor this singular accomplishment until he had dealt with a colorful rogue whose rare but squandered gifts nearly proved a match for his own. Unlike a number of lesser criminals, William Chaloner has been denied his rightful place in the *Dictionary of National Biography*, for this more mature and cunning forerunner of the Artful Dodger long succeeded in making fools of the highest officials of the land while simultaneously masterminding a notorious ring of clippers and counterfeiters.

The world into which Newton entered in pursuit of

the criminal element was that immortalized by John Gay in *The Beggar's Opera*. His many contacts, any one of whom might have done him in as he moved about London, included murderers, thieves, prostitutes, beggars, and perjurers—the socially dispossessed and the mentally unbalanced. He learned of bribes to destroy evidence, of hideaways in outlying villages, of clandestine meetings in taverns and garrets. He developed contacts with men and women of many aliases. Those who refused to cooperate were brought before him at the Mint, located in the infamous Tower of London, to be interrogated in chains. While Newton himself stayed within the law, the moral level of those with whom he dealt soon convinced him that its provisions had to be bent—if not broken—in the service of a higher morality.

A natural-born swindler, Chaloner first made his way in the city by fashioning worthless tin watches, which he hawked in the streets for whatever the gullible would pay. He soon gained an accomplice, and together they set up for what Chaloner himself described as "Piss-Pot Prophets, or Quack-Doctors." The turning point in his career came when he bribed a japanner to teach him the finisher's art. With this knowledge he undertook the gilding of coins, which in turn brought him to the deeper study of metals and the counterfeiting of guineas and pistoles. Within two years' time William Chaloner was a rich man, dining off silver plate and riding about the streets of London in an elegant carriage with a beautiful mistress.

Yet wealth and the false respectability it purchased were less important to this high-stakes gambler than the playing of the game. Chaloner loved the grand design— the plotting, the trickery, the fraud he called "funning," the manipulation of pawns, but most of all the intellectual sleight-of-hand that pitted his wits against the combined talents and resources of officialdom. When confronted with evidence linking him to a major crime, he consistently wriggled free by resorting to the big lie, a strategem he jokingly referred to as "bubbling." By the time he crossed swords with the master of the Mint, Chaloner was effervescent.

Reveling in the battle of wits to come, I was liberated at long last from the mathematics and science that had chained me to Newton for nearly 400 pages. Like Dr. Watson, I joined my Holmes in the exhilarating pursuit of his Moriarty, feeling myself a participant in the drama for the first time. Chaloner struck a major blow by convincing a committee of Parliament, over Newton's strenuous objections, to consider the charlatan's recommendations for improvements in the minting of new coin. Soon Chaloner hatched yet another scheme by which he aimed to fun the government out of £1,000. Assisted by one Aubrey Price, he concocted a preposterous story of a Jacobite plot to seize Dover Castle. The two declared themselves willing to risk life and limb in the service of the crown by posing as secret agents for the purpose of compiling a list of suspected traitors. Adding insult to injury, Chaloner taunted "that old Dogg" Newton, who, in a fit of anger, vowed to hang the villain. It was at this point that legal niceties were abandoned.

With his nemesis under arrest and safely locked up within Newgate's stone walls, Newton adopted a strategy now commonly referred to as entrapment. He employed three convicts to gain Chaloner's confidence and pass on his criminal admissions. The ending, which had been so slow in coming, lasted but three weeks. Chaloner went on trial for high treason and was found guilty, owing largely to the testimony of several witnesses, felons all, who were allowed to recount the events of the past six years with little regard for specifics as to time and place.

That Chaloner was guilty of many crimes is indisputable, but my conscience, unlike Newton's, began to waver over the methods employed to bring the rogue to justice. The prisoner's constitutional rights notwithstanding, Newton believed that the condemned had gotten exactly what he deserved. "Criminals, like dogs," he once remarked, "always return to their vomit."[10]

Many are of this same opinion three centuries later, especially where drug dealers, organized crime, and violent offenders are concerned. Was Newton's attitude right for his time, which was far less sensitive to civil rights, yet wrong for our own? I have never resolved this question, but I remain haunted by a sentence from one of Chaloner's last letters, written to Newton himself shortly before his scheduled execution: "I am going to be murdered although perhaps you may think not but tis true I shall be murdered by the worst of all murders that is in the face of Justice unless I am rescued by your merciful hands."[11] Days later Chaloner got his answer; he was loaded onto a cart and paraded through the streets to the gallows in Hyde Park. There he repeated his claim, crying out hysterically to the assembled throng that he was being murdered by perjury and injustice. Few took notice, for rare was the criminal who claimed otherwise. It was not by chance that I titled the chapter containing this not so simple tale of good and evil "A Morality Play."

What, then, is this thing biographers and their fellow historians call objectivity? A chimera some would say, and in their defense I propose the following scenario. Suppose that every scrap of information on Abraham Lincoln could somehow be collected in a single repository. Further imagine that three biographers are chosen to enter that repository and, without benefit of collaboration, produce three separate lives of the man.

Let us even suppose that our biographers are the same age and sex, come from similar socio-economic backgrounds, have even studied at the same university under a common mentor, specializing in nineteenth-century American history. Would their respective lives of Lincoln be identical, or even nearly so?

Barbara Tuchman, who decries the use of any sources other than primary, nevertheless writes of the need to form one's materials into "a developing dramatic narrative."[12] Yet how many lives, including those of the great, unfold in spectacular fashion? Once known in detail, the daily existence of novelists, statesmen, feminists, artists, even warriors, are not so extraordinary when measured against their fellow beings; the skill of the biographer only makes it appear so. It was for this very reason that Dr. Johnson stressed the practical value of biography, arguing that it appealed to the average reader more directly than history because all individuals are essentially alike and therefore identify with those about whom they read. In theory anyone's life, if dramatically recounted, would be of interest, for prince and pauper experience the same pain.

And what of the biographer who, in the guise of objectivity, informs his readers that the figures in the narrative "have been allowed to speak for themselves"? Someone, presumably the author, decided which lines to quote or to omit, which gestures to play up or to play down, which descriptive details to retain or to cut. Few, if any, of these matters would be handled in the same way by our three imaginary biographers, and so it is in the real world where peoples' lives are written by those with highly diverse backgrounds. While I view with deep suspicion that literary import from France known as deconstructionism, which argues that the author's use of words rather than his intent reveals all, there is no denying that semantics, vocabulary, and style are as important as the selection process itself. Individual as the human fingerprint, they provide an absolute guarantee that a life will never be written the same way twice; and while the word definitive has no place in biography, where fixed and final portraits are merely illusions, the best writer is usually the best biographer. To readers of our vanishing century Mark Twain is inseparable from the voice of Justin Kaplan, the young Theodore Roosevelt from Edmund Morris, Truman from David Mc-Cullough, Crazy Horse from Mari Sandoz, Churchill from William Manchester. Each of these lives will be rewritten in the century to come, perhaps several times over, but hardly to greater literary effect.

It is clear that when the biographer speaks of objectivity, he is not referring to that wisdom of the universe to which a dumb-struck Job yielded when challenged by Yahweh to explain the secrets of creation. Objectivity to the biographer means that one recognizes the importance of impartiality and the danger in becoming too closely identified with one's subject, a standard aspired to but never achieved in the absolute. Nor, on deeper reflection, would we wish it so. An historian without an informed opinion is tantamount to an automaton, and unreadable besides.

To date, I have tended to view my own relationships with my subjects as kaleidoscopic, one more akin to the workings of the judicial process than Holmes's concept of partnership or Oates's profound bonding. On a given morning, when the writing is going well, I may assume any number of courtroom roles in hopes of obtaining the answers I require: witness (friendly or hostile), prosecutor, counsel for the defense, judge, juror, or simply spectator. This is not to say that my method, any more than theirs or the proceedings it emulates, is neutral. What I seek is that critical sum of evidence that will

and subject are responsible for their actions, that a moral continuity exists between the inner and outer person. If this is not objectivity, it is as close as biography is likely to come.

2

Isaac Newton's Hair

The scientific procedures used in the testing of the rare laboratory samples were as follows:

(i) *Neutron Activation Analysis*
    The individual untreated hairs were irradiated in the Herald reactor located at the Atomic Weapons Research Establishment, Aldermaston.
    (a) *Sodium, Chlorine, Manganese, Bromine, Zinc, Gold and Mercury.*
        After a 30 minute or 5 day (mercury and gold) irradiation the hairs were counted in a gamma spectrometer. The complex spectra were resolved and the results calculated by computer . . .

(ii) *Atomic Absorption Spectrophotometry*
    (a) *Lead*
        The lead analyses were performed using a Perkin-Elmer atomic absorption spectrophotometer equipped with a HGA-70 furnace atomiser. Centimetre lengths of hair were introduced into the furnace, the organic matter destroyed and the lead absorption signal recorded.[1]

The resulting print-out proved no less impressive than the method of analysis. Whereas the mean level of

19

lead in the hair of an English adult is 24 parts per million (ppm), the samples in question yielded readings of 132 and 191 ppm, more than enough to inflict significant neurological damage. Additional injury might well have been sustained from the inordinate concentrations of mercury or quicksilver. Neutron analysis produced readings of 54 and a staggering 197 ppm compared to a mean figure of 5.1 ppm. On the basis of this data alone one might reasonably deduce that the subject was as mad as the felt hatters who used copious amounts of the heavy metal in their trade. Indeed, the researchers conducting their medical diagnosis by historical fiat come very close to saying as much in their tersely worded conclusion:

> Thus the unusually high concentration in Newton's hair of heavy metals known to produce nervous symptoms is strong circumstantial evidence in favor of the hypothesis that Newton's so-called 'nervous breakdown' of 1692/93 was due principally to poisoning by the metals which he used so frequently and with such cavalier disregard for his own safety in his chemical experiments.[2]

Not until 1689, when Isaac Newton was in his forty-seventh year, did he commission Godfrey Kneller to paint his first and most famous portrait. At the height of his mental powers and poised on the threshold of international fame, the author of the *Principia mathematica* had recently left Cambridge's Trinity College for London, where he took a seat as a Whig backbencher in the historic Convention Parliament. Newton's silver mane is thick and flowing, the myopic eyes somewhat protuberant but piercing, the angular chin deeply cleft, the mouth sensuous and delicately formed. The long thin fingers of the right hand, which extend from beneath the subject's academic gown, are suggestive of a virtuoso of another kind, a performer of music rather than the revolutionary choreographer of matter's deterministic dance. In sum, Kneller's midlife portrait is a foreshadowing of that famous Jovian look borne by the aged Newton, who shared with Einstein the aspect of one present at the Creation.

During Newton's later years, his nephew-in-law, John Conduitt, described the savant as possessing a lively and piercing eye, with a fine head of hair as white as silver. "When his peruke was off [it] was a venerable sight." Dr. William Stukeley, a member of the great man's inner circle, quaintly attributed the condition to a hot and dry constitution.

Almost all that is known of Newton's physical appearance as a young man is that he was of about medium stature and had turned prematurely gray by the age of thirty. John Wickins, his Trinity chamberfellow of nearly two decades, half teasingly told him it was "ye Effect of his deep attention of Mind," to which a normally staid Newton jokingly replied that he experimented so frequently with quicksilver "as from thence he took so soon the Colour."[3]

As the researchers themselves point out, the ideal way of testing their medical hypothesis would have been through chemical analysis of the bodily remains, a course fraught with overwhelming obstacles. Newton's final resting place, which had been denied to several men of noble birth, was chosen for its prominence in the nave of Westminster Abbey. The huge monument commissioned by the heirs was completed four years later in 1731, a baroque monstrosity replete with cherubs clutching emblems of his greatest discoveries. "Let Mortals rejoyce That there has existed such and so great an Ornament to the Human Race." Needless to say, the prospect that a piece of that ornament, however miniscule, would be provided scientists by exhumation of the skeleton—assuming the bones survive—was virtually nonexistent.

It so happened that Louis Trenchard More, Newton's first major biographer of this century, had been shown a lock of the natural philosopher's hair while doing research at Hurstbourne Park, the Portsmouth family seat, in the early 1930s. More described it as "silver white and unusually fine in texture."[4] The Portsmouths had come into possession of this and much other Newtoniana, including the invaluable scientific papers, via Catherine Barton, Newton's beautiful and witty niece who lived with her uncle in London for many years before marrying Conduitt, Newton's eventual successor as master of the Mint. Their only child, also named Catherine, wed John Wallop, the first Earl of Portsmouth. In all likelihood, it was Lady Wallop's mother who preserved the telltale lock.

Nothing of this was known to me when, in 1978, I arrived at Cambridge in the dead of winter to begin research on a biography of Newton. One blustery afternoon found me huddled over a space heater at Trinity's three-hundred-year-old Wren Library while examining some of the 600 or so volumes once owned by Newton himself. A tap on the shoulder jerked me back into the twentieth century. There stood a half-smiling Trevor Kaye, the angular sublibrarian who spent his evenings playing jazz saxophone at a local nightclub, thus dashing one of my many stereotypes of English bibliophiles. He placed a box on the oak table at which I was working. "These items belonged to Newton, or so tradition holds, and I thought his would-be biographer should have a look at them." With that, he turned on his heels and disappeared down the great marble corridor, leaving an unguarded scholar with a treasure more dear than Spanish gold.

Among the items in the box were some small scientific instruments, an ink bottle or two whose liquid contents had long since reverted to black powder, and a little heart-shaped case bearing the typed label, "Lock of hair from the head of Isaac Newton." Whether my hands were trembling, I do not remember, but I opened the container to gaze upon nature's equivalent of spun silver, a commodity long dreamt of by the alchemists of old. The ethereal lock was composed of dozens of individual hairs, each iridescent in the pale light filtering through the Wren's great mullioned windows.

Suddenly, the voice that a mischievous boy's parents continually warn him against came alive. "Take just one for yourself," it intoned, "hide it in your handkerchief! There were so many that nobody will ever know. You deserve it; you have crossed an ocean and contracted walking pneumonia for Newton's sake. Go on, hide it in your handkerchief!"

Even as I sat there, wrestling with a suspect conscience, three hairs from the box before me, along with eleven others from the Portsmouth estate, were about to be immolated in the interests of medical science, an irony Newton, who was both a true believer and a consummate experimenter would have relished.

As with so many facets of his intellectual development, the turning point in his study of alchemy had come at Trinity College before his swift rise to the rank of Lucasian Professor. The so-called "philosophical notebook," which encompasses his private thoughts as a Cambridge undergraduate, contains guidelines on how to make a crucible by coating it with a mixture of "tobaccopipe clay & salt of Tartar."[5] He further paused to contemplate the virtues of "Fier" and its byproduct "Heate," and wrote five pages on "Attomes," seven on "Motion," and three on "Matter" in addition to describing "Attraction," both magnetic and an electrical, "Flux and Reflux," "Sympathy and Antipathie," "Density," and Filtracion." Here was the true seed of the alchemy, if not the flower.

In this endeavor, as in all others, Newton would not rest until the tracks of his erudition were spread across an endless succession of pages. Humphrey Newton, a distant relative who served as his laboratory assistant during the 1680s, described his employer as

> So intent, so serious upon his studies yt he eat very sparingly, nay ofttimes he has forgot to eat at all. He very rarely went to Bed, till 2 or 3 of ye Clock, sometimes not till 5 or 6, lying about 4 or 5 hours, especially at spring & fall of ye Leaf, at wch Times he used to imploy about 6 weeks in his Elaboratory, the fire scarcely going out either Night or Day, he sitting up one Night, as I did another till he had finished his Chymicall Experiments, in ye Performance of wch he was ye most accurate, strict, exact. What his Aim might be, I was not able to penetrate into, but his Pains, his Diliginc at those sett Times made me think, he aimed at something beyond ye Reach of humane Art & Industry.[6]

Although he was no Boswell, Humphrey well knew that he was in the presence, if not the company, of abstracted genius impelled by an intense moral force, a man who could never accept John Donne's indictment of the emergent modern world: " 'Tis all in peeces, all cohaerence gone."

Newton's Puritan sense of mission was nothing if not absolute, and never was it more evident than when he immersed himself in the alchemist's art. He was well into his eighties when he informed Conduitt, "They who search after the Philosopher's Stone by their own rules [are] obliged to a strict & religious life."[7] But let there be no misunderstanding: he neither heard voices nor considered himself a vessel waiting to receive holy text. As ever, Newton appealed to an overarching principle of cosmic order. In one sense he was enthralled by the very questions that so enliven current scientific debate. Black holes, those Dantean pits in the firmament, are intriguing partly because their explanation promises to aid in the unification of the great and the small. The crucial theories of twentieth-century physics are relativity, which is played out across the numbing void of trackless space, and quantum mechanics, which seeks to open up invisible worlds of streaking micromatter. The great problem is to formulate a principle that fuses the two, which has thus far eluded all aspirants, including a deeply frustrated Einstein. Newton too sought a grand synthesis, the wedding of the microcosm to the macrocosm to forge an even more magnificent habitable creation—a *science universelle*. As an alchemist and favorite of the Lord, he attempted nothing less than a "metascientific" synthesis, from the Greek word meaning beyond. That he was destined for supreme disappointment cannot be doubted.

Nothing is known of the actions and events that directly preceded the dark passage of September 1693, when, on the thirteenth, Newton wrote the following to Samuel Pepys, the incomparable diarist.

Sir,

Some time after Mr. Millington [a Fellow of Magdalene College, Cambridge] had delivered your message, he pressed me to see you the next time I went to London. I was averse; but upon his pressing consented, before I considered what I did, for I am extremely troubled at the embroilment I am in, and have neither slept well this twelve month, nor have my former consistency of mind. I never designed to get anything by your interests, nor by King James's favour, but am now sensible that I must withdraw from your acquaintance and see neither you nor the rest of my friends any more, if I may but leave them quietly. I beg your pardon for saying I would see you again, and rest your most humble and obedient servant.

> *Is. Newton*[8]

Pepys was not only deeply shaken by Newton's allegations, he was innocent on all counts. The former Secretary to the Admiralty had been forced to retire during the Glorious Revolution and was lately living in virtual seclusion while attempting to sort through his voluminous papers. If he wielded any influence at court it was of the negative and therefore useless kind, although Newton, in alluding to the exiled James II, seems to have imagined that time and history had turned back upon themselves, as when Alice passed through the looking glass.

Three days later, on September 16, Newton's unsettling letter to Pepys was followed by an even more disturbing and vengeful one to political philosopher John Locke. It was dispatched from the Bull Inn in Shoreditch, London. What Newton was doing there he did not say.

Sr

Being of opinion that you endeavoured to embroil me with woemen & by other means I was so much affected with it as that when one told me you were sickly & would not live I answered twere better if you were dead. I desire you to forgive me this uncharitableness. For I am now satisfied that what you have done is just & beg your pardon for having hard thoughts of you for it & for representing that you struck at ye root of morality in a principle that you laid down in your book of Ideas & designed to

pursue in another book & that I took you for a
Hobbist. I beg your pardon also for saying or thinking that there was a designe to sell me an office, or
to embroile me, I am

your most humble & most
unfortunate Servant
Is. Newton[9]

A most unfortunate servant indeed. A severely deluded,
if not paranoid, Newton, now in his fifty-first year, had
accused his loyal admirers of conspiring against him,
referred to conversations and visits that had never taken
place, and sought to sever his hard-won contacts with
the outside world. Sick of mind, he was no less sick of
heart.

To their lasting credit, both Pepys and Locke displayed great compassion. John Millington assured Pepys
that he had delivered no message to Newton of any
kind. Then, at Pepys's urging, he took the added pre-
caution of visiting Newton's chambers on the twenty-
eighth. His host anticipated the reason for the call
because Millington had said nothing before Newton
confessed to have written Pepys "a very odd letter." He
blamed his illness on "a distemper that much seized his
head, and that kept him awake for five nights together."
Newton begged Pepys's forgiveness, "He being very
much ashamed." So far as Millington could tell, there
was no reason to suspect that Newton had taken permanent leave of his senses, though he observed that the
natural philosopher remained under some small degree
of melancholy.[10]

"[Give] me leave to assure you that I am more ready
to forgive you than you can be to desire it," a hopeful
Locke replied on October 5, "and I do it soe freely and
fully yt I wish for noe thing more than the opportunities

to convince you that I truly love & esteem you & yt I have still the same good will for you as if noe thing of this had happened."[11] But by the time Locke's letter reached Cambridge the crisis had passed. The only explanation Newton could offer Locke for his bizarre conduct was a somewhat more detailed account of what Millington had learned a fortnight earlier:

> The last winter by sleeping often by my fire I got an ill habit of sleeping & a distemper wch this summer has been epidemical put me further out of order, so that when I wrote to you I had not slept an hour for a fortnight together & for 5 nights together not a wink. I remember I wrote to you but what I said of your book I remember not. If you please to send me a transcript of that passage I will give you an account of it if I can.[12]

The factors that impinged upon the mental equilibrium of Isaac Newton are many and virtually impossible to disentangle. No one can be absolutely certain—three centuries after the event—as to which of them plunged him into the depths of psychic chaos. Yet any conscientious biographer who has lived with the man for several years would find it impossible to ardently embrace the poisoning hypothesis, however seductive.

To begin with, Newton's own description of his malady is lacking in detail, nor did he himself see a cause-and-effect relationship between his illness and alchemical experimentation. On the contrary, he thought himself the victim of a "distempter" of "epidemical" proportions. While the term meant many things to people of the seventeenth century, distemper was hardly associated with mercury or lead poisoning. This would have been especially true in Newton's case, for as the most accomplished alchemist of his day, he knew full well the considerable risks associated with the tasting of metallic compounds and the breathing of their fumes in an unventilated chamber. His jest to Wickins that his hair had turned silver prematurely from working with mercury tells us that much. Knowing the hazards, against which he admittedly took few precautions, he would have also known the symptoms, many of which had been meticulously documented by Paracelsus in the sixteenth century.

Indeed, the very scientific data cited by those espousing the poisoning theory can be countered with equally credible medical evidence, or rather a lack of it. Among the most prominent symptoms of mercury poisoning is a tremor afflicting the hands, a condition immortalized in literature by the shy Oxford mathematician Charles Lutwidge Dodgson, whose pen name was Lewis Carroll. One might reasonably expect Newton's handwriting to reflect such a condition at the time of his breakdown, but it does not. Ulceration of the gums and loosening of the teeth are also symptoms common to mercury poisoning, yet Conduitt informs us that when Newton died at the age of eighty-four he possessed all of his secondary teeth but one, a remarkable achievement for an octogenarian of any day, let alone a seventeenth-century fancier of sweets. Numerous other pronounced symptoms received no mention, whether by Newton himself or by those who shared his company: jaundice, emaciation, flaking skin, darkened nails, premature aging, weight loss (Newton inclined toward corpulence in later life), lethargy, let alone visual impairment, convulsions, coma, and paralysis. Uremia attendant on kidney failure is one of the common consequences of mercury poisoning, but the record is no less mute on this score. Most important of all, perhaps, is Newton's exceedingly rapid and apparently complete recovery at a time when alchemy continued to occupy him more than any other pursuit. As the laboratory analysis so graphically illustrates, heavy metals, like country cousins, can be pesky visitants, refusing to take their leave even centuries after a natural death. Thus, there should have been additional breakdowns, given Newton's prolonged addiction to the fire and the crucible. Yet the only other mental disturbance to be documented with certainty occurred in 1664, well before alchemical experimentation had become part of his life, when he suffered from exhaustion and disorientation brought on by observing comets the night long.

The Newton we have come to know was famous for the clarity and persuasiveness of his scientific reasoning, the profundity of the questions he addressed to nature. No conundrum seemed too knotty for him to untangle, no phenomenon too obscure to ponder. The cold blood of stolid yeomen, lawyers, and Puritan clerics coursed through his veins; his logic was unsullied by emotion. Then came Nicolas Fatio de Dullier, a young and gifted Swiss mathematician, to whom he was drawn as to a sympathetic powder. Never in his adult life had he experienced such a broad and frightening range of emotions, rejoicing in anticipation of their every meeting, despairing when Fatio left for Europe and then, after his return, hesitated to reside with him at Cambridge. When Fatio became ill Newton also started to ail. He informed Pepys that his insomnia and poor appetite, both of which played roles in his derangement, had lasted a *year*. Significantly, word of Fatio's sickness arrived in a letter dated November 17, 1692, while Newton's letter to Pepys announcing his own infirmity is dated September 13, 1693. And though we can never know for certain, Newton's mysterious visit to London from where he wrote his curious letter to Locke could well have been the occasion of his final shattering rendezvous with Fatio.

The letters also attest to Newton's difficulty in making his existence known to the nonscientific world. He had convinced himself that the post of warden of the Mint was an entitlement of which he was being wrongfully deprived, an extension of his conspiracy theory of history which, among other things, cast the Roman Catholic Church in the role of Revelations' blasphemous Whore of Babylon. To make matters worse, the lion had groveled like a common peasant before lesser mortals, such as Locke's patrons Lord and Lady Masham ("embroil me with woemen"), in order to obtain what was his by right of accomplishment. Others seemed in control of his destiny, an unacceptable violation of his obsession with absolute freedom of action. After visiting with Newton, Millington lamented to Pepys that *"it was a sign of how much it [learning] is looked after, when such a person as Mr. Newton lies so neglected by those in power."*[13] In underscoring this passage, Millington was keenly aware that the natural philosopher, who had forgotten much else following his recovery, remained deeply aggrieved over what seemed to him a never ending wrong.

Finally, the biographer must demur when it is alleged that the breakdown of 1693 occurred during a period relatively free of intense mental exertion, a seeming hiatus following the *Principia*'s release.[14] When no government appointment was forthcoming, Newton sat down at his desk one last time in the hope of restoring his connection with some divine source, a proven cure for rejection in the past. The last of his prodigous reserves were thrown into a final assault in an effort to achieve an even more comprehensive understanding of the natural order. Writing, in May 1694, to Nathaniel Hawes, treasurer of Christ's Hospital in London, he asserted, "A Vulgar Mechanick can practice what he has been taught or seen done, but if he is in an error, he knows not how to find it out and correct it, Whereas he that is able to reason nimbly and judiciously about figure, force, and motion, is never at rest till he gets over every rub."[15]

The highly creative individual looks with greater fondness on what he pursues than on what he possesses, on what he dreams of doing than on what he has done. Newton had spent the last three decades of his life tracing the mazelike ridges in the fingerprint of God, only to discover a *cul-de-sac* at their center that barred any prospect of effecting the grand synthesis of his imagination. He had, in Stukeley's words, "unfolded the economy of the macrocosm," but the secret of the microcosm still eluded him. His work in alchemy reached its febrile climax, if not quite its end, at the very moment of his breakdown, when he metaphorically immolated himself on Vulcan's altar. Working at the ragged edge in the spring and summer of 1693, he completed five chapters of a manuscript titled *Praxis*, his projected magnum opus on the multiplication of metals. For a brief time the secret of the ages seemed within his grasp, as it had some twenty years earlier when gold mixed with purified quicksilver had sprouted, swelled, and branched on being exposed to fire. But as before, disillusionment set in, at first manifesting itself in cancelled passages, finally in the complete abandonment of the work.

For the first time in his life Newton had to face up to something he had always known but never fully wanted to admit: that there exists in the world nothing physical to account for the world—for the drive of elemental particles to become flesh and bone, for the primoridal balance between undulating sea and steadfast shore, for hurtling planet and anchored star. Having forever banished certain of nature's mysteries, he had also exposed the glaring limitations of the mechanical philosophy, a science that had failed him for the first time. The shadows temporarily enveloped him, obliterating the line between illusion and reality. In a crushing fall of arrogance, Isaac Newton lost the secret confidence of God, shattering his self-myth and stemming the wellsprings of his creativity. The mind was still intact, but the spirit was no longer willing. He who had attempted to rise above human art and industry longed to be shed of Cambridge lest someone discover his terrible secret.

Such are the elusive factors no X-ray can illuminate, no reactor can count, no graph can plot on a computer print-out. Newton eventually secured the post he was seeking, leaving Cambridge for London town and the Mint on March 23, 1696.

It was a much different London that I flew out of on a warm April morning 286 years later, having done with Cambridge myself, though for very different reasons. The great struggle with the blank page now lay before me, yet I was buoyed by my personal encounter with the iridescent remnant of the man Edmond Halley aptly celebrated as being nearest to the gods. I imagined myself, when the writing was going poorly, taking out a delicate silver box lined in red satin—Newton's favorite color—to gaze down upon a tiny strand of immortality. I imagined . . . I still imagine. For in the event you are wondering how I fared with my suspect conscience, I departed Cambridge with nothing more than my notes, my luggage, and an empty handkerchief.

3

Whither Fatio?

Every great man has his disciples, Oscar Wilde once observed, and it is usually Judas who writes his biography. Even when no attempt has been made to keep the less ennobling facts of a life secret, the psychological barriers facing the biographer can be formidable. Witness Barbara Tuchman's difficulties in coming to grips with the subject of her Pulitzer Prize-winning biography, General Joseph Stilwell, whose nickname, "Vinegar Joe," was as well deserved as his chestfull of campaign ribbons. Tuchman, who was brought up in a protected world free of four-letter words and scatalogical images, was shaken on being faced with Stilwell's uninhibited use of nonparlor language in his diary. Even more upsetting were the General's racial slurs—on a good day Chiang Kai-shek was merely dismissed as "The Peanut"—and "horrid" references to President Roosevelt as "Rubberlegs." After agonizing with her writer's conscience, the biographer finally decided on an unpalatable but necessary modus operandi. Though it felt like picking up a cockroach, "wicked nicknames" went into the record, while certain of the vulgar language did not. "I eventually worked around that problem by a generalized, if nonspecific, reference to Stilwell's vocabulary." Looking back on what she had done several years later, the author felt that perhaps she had taken the problem too seriously, especially in light of the relentless assault on language during the decade of the seventies. "I had no idea how common and banal these words were in male conversation."[1]

Tuchman has written with more than passing conviction of her "instinctive sense" of personal privacy—a conviction which has also informed her art: "I feel no great obligation to pry into a subject's private life and reveal—unless it is clearly relevant—what he wanted to keep private. Do we really have to know of some famous person that he wet his pants at age six and practiced oral sex at sixty?" Shakespeare, after all, would still be Shakespeare and Hamlet a vacillating prince even if we had knowledge that such were the bard's excretory and amatory propensities.[2]

Echoes of Alfred Lord Tennyson defending a less circumspect peer of the realm. "What business has the public to know of Byron's wildnesses? He has given them fine work and they ought to be satisfied." Whether, at that particular moment, the author of *In Memoriam* was pondering his own biographical fate once he had crossed the bar is not certain. However, as a profound spokesman for the ideas and values of his time, Tennyson captured perfectly the Victorian attitude toward biography. The writer of the life was obligated to maintain a narrow focus, highlighting only the exemplary acts of exemplary beings. It mattered not whether he was chronicling the life of a true saint like Francis of Assisi or a secular one like Henry David Thoreau. No hint of flaking plaster was permitted to show through; the door of almost every respectable publisher was barred to the would-be iconoclast. If one aspired to membership in the club, he must never, in the words of Victorian biographer John Morley, "contemplate the hinder parts of their divinities."

Still, the famous felt endangered. A culture's values change. The idealizing word sculptor might one day be replaced by the realist unwilling to genuflect before his subject, thus allowing pigeons to violate the pedestal. "The field of literary history," as Marc Pachter observes, "is thick with the smoke of burning leaves."[3] Tempted by the fire, Dickens reduced two decades of his private life to ash within minutes; Henry James doubled that sacrifice in another metaphoric act of self-mutilation. Though less dramatic, T.S. Eliot spoke more directly to the point: "I do not wish my executors," he admonished in a codicil to his will, "to facilitate or countenance the writing of a biography of me." Finally, as Pachter points out, even Walt Whitman, who pledged Horace Traubel, his nineteenth-century "Boswell," to "write about me honest," including "all the hells and damns," fed the fires while telling tall tales to cover his mighty tracks, not the least of reasons for titling his most remembered poem "Song of Myself."

> *I celebrate and sing myself*
> *And what I assume, you shall assume . . .*

As I learned from my own archival research and interviews, Loren Eiseley, with the cooperation of both his wife and research assistant, purged his files of much biographical grist. Then, within days of his death, the writer's nephew fulfilled a long-standing promise. The young man went down into the basement of the Eiseleys' apartment building and began hauling away the heavy boxes of papers his uncle had told him to destroy. These he burned, claiming not to have examined the contents before the sacrifice. Curiously, almost tragicomically for one who was a close observer rather than a major actor, Eiseley had referred to Hemingway's treatment by biographers when exacting his nephew's pledge.

The surviving correspondence attests to the fact that there were several who aspired to write Eiseley's life, but

he managed to keep them at arm's length. The shell
formed in childhood had thickened and grown en-
crusted over the years; it rarely opened and closed
quickly. It was one thing if he himself chose to reveal
certain secrets from his past, but it was forbidden that
anyone else come prying around. He thought of biography, when he thought of it at all, in nineteenth-
century terms—the Victorian lionization of the public
man. The "new biography," as it has been called by
Leon Edel in *Writing Lives*, his boldly subtitled *Principia
Biographica*, was simply more than Eiseley could tolerate,
what with its seeming obsession with sex, fascination for
idle gossip, and dime store psychoanalysis. It was another product of a "permissive society," amounting to
little more than removing someone's clothes before a
gaping public. Finally, there was the pride of the thinking man, the belief that no one could possibly capture
his essence on the flat plain of the printed page, the
biographical equivalent of caveat emptor.

I would like to think that had I been in Barbara
Tuchman's shoes the brutal language employed by Stilwell would have shocked me too. Yet I must also be
candid and admit that this male historian of a later
generation would have doubtless quoted the general
verbatim, hoping all the while that my mother would
not ask to see the manuscript while visiting over the
holidays.

The biographer's decision of whether or not to use
an unedifying or controversial episode from the life of
his subject is not only a matter of taste but one of
objectives. "In so far as I have used biography in my
work," Tuchman writes, "it has been less for the sake of
the individual subject than as a vehicle for exhibiting an
age, as in the case of Coucy in *A Distant Mirror*; or a
country and its state of mind, as in the case of Speaker
Reed and Richard Strauss in *The Proud Tower*; or an

historic situation, as in the case of *Stilwell and the American Experience in China*."[4] Fair enough. But what of the biographer whose objectives are less macrocosmic, the artist and scholar who is primarily concerned with what one writer has termed the "inner myth" as opposed to the grand public experience?[5]

As it happened, Isaac Newton wet his pants, though whether at the age of six I cannot say. The inventory taken of the natural philosopher's possessions just after his demise lists only two suits among the articles of apparel, a meager wardrobe indeed for a man of great wealth and prominence. This revelation prompted Newton scholar Richard de Villamil to quip, "This looks like one set on and the other at the wash."[6]

While Newton was not a man who threw money around, the solution to this minor mystery probably has little to do with a Puritan bent for tight-fistedness. In 1723, after becoming seriously ill, the president of the Royal Society and master of the Mint quit dosing himself, as he had done all his life, and sought the services of Richard Mead and William Cheselden, two of London's most respected physicians. After first attributing their patient's problem to the stone, they later issued a revised diagnosis. Newton, who was now in his eighties, was afflicted by a weakness of the sphinter. He suffered the humiliation of incontinence of the bladder from this time on, forcing him to give up his carriage for the less unsettling motion of a sedan chair. He also ceased dining abroad with friends and rarely entertained at home. We may reasonably conclude that the toll taken on his social life was matched by the attrition of a once fine wardrobe.

Of this unfortunate condition, I wrote no more than a sentence or two, but of Tuchman's other concern; namely, the sexual proclivities of one's subject, I had considerably more to say—hopefully for good reason.

After coming under Mead's care, the aged Newton confided that he had never violated chastity and would die a virgin, or so a gossipy Voltaire, who later interviewed Mead at some length, noted in his *Letters Concerning the English Nation*. Word of this moral victory was also communicated to the poet Thomas Maude by an elderly relative of Newton's, who had allegedly learned of it from the great man himself.[7] The intriguing question raised by this statement is not whether it applies to members of the opposite sex, for there is little doubt in my mind that it does, but to those of Newton's gender as well, most particularly a gifted young mathematician from the Swiss province of Vaud.

Newton's work habits, both in early life and in middle age, were pathological in their addictiveness. He starved himself socially, sexually, and, not least, nutritionally, courting sickness, failure, even insanity to test whether the established world would break him or whether he would triumph by displacing certain of its time-worn fundaments with new ones of his own. John North, the eccentric but perceptive master of Cambridge's Trinity College, once remarked to his nephew that "if Sir Isaac Newton had not wrought with his hands in making experiments, he had killed himself with study. A man may so engage his mind as almost to forget he hath a body which must be waited upon and served."[8]

Almost—but not quite. In a history of the Church begun in the late 1670s, Newton, who was living the life of a secular monastic, opened a rare psychological window through which one can survey his ongoing struggle to keep the Devil and the demons of lust at arm's length.

> The way to chastity is not to struggle directly with incontinent thoughts but to avert ye thoughts by some imployment, or by reading, or meditating on other things, or by

convers. By immoderate fasting the body is also put out
of its due temper & and for want of sleep the fansy is
invigorated . . . & by degrees inclines towards a delirium
so much that those Monks who fasted most arrived to a
state of seeing apparitions of woemen & their shapes &
of hearing their voices in such a lively manner as made
them often think the visions true apparitions of ye Devil.
Thus while we pray that God would not lead us into
temptation these men ran themselves headlong into it.[9]

Nicolas Fatio de Dullier remains a fascinating
enigma, as he was to Isaac Newton, his most intimate
acquaintance of the early 1690s. Fatio burst upon London society with the aura, almost, of a Magus, yet he
eventually wound up in the pillory at Charing Cross, an
unmourned victim of his indiscreet espousal of hetero-
dox theology.

If one is to judge by the youthful portrait that hangs
in Geneva's University Library, the Fatio Newton came
to know was far from a handsome man. The countenance is dominated by a great Roman nose made even
more prominent by a high, sweeping forehead, diminutive mouth, and rather sharply pointed chin. Only the
eyes are compelling. Keen and intelligent, accentuated
by steeply arched brows and high cheekbones, they
seem capable of transfixing anyone who might come
too near.

The powerful attraction experienced between the
middle-aged bachelor and his much younger admirer is
perhaps best described as infatuation. The earliest surviving letter, dated October 1689, is in Newton's hand.
He was about to leave Cambridge for London: "I . . .
should be very glad to be in ye same lodging with you. I
will bring my books & your letters with me."[10] Fatio's
reply is lost, but his feelings toward Newton were expressed in no uncertain terms in a November letter to
Jean-Robert Chouet, his friend and onetime professor

of philosophy at Geneva. How wonderful it would be, he rhapsodized, to become a permanent citizen of England and to inhabit the same dwelling as Newton, who was both the greatest mathematician ever to have lived and the most worthy gentleman he had ever met. The Cartesian system was finished, no matter what others might think. "Its all over for vortices . . . which were only an empty imagination." If the money were but available, he, Nicolas Fatio de Dullier, would erect great and lasting monuments to his godlike friend. Posterity would then know that Newton had at least one contemporary who recognized his true worth.[11]

The two spent as much time together as was possible during the next year, after which Fatio sailed for Europe, where he remained for fifteen months. When Newton heard nothing from him for "ye half year," he could suppress his anxiety no longer and inquired after his friend in a letter to John Locke. Coming from anyone else, this would seem a matter of little import, but Isaac Newton almost never asked after an acquaintance—no matter how learned or influential. Fatio returned to London early in September 1691. He promptly wrote Christiaan Huygens, the great Dutch scientist, that Newton would be arriving in the capital in a very few days. It was just as Fatio said it would be. Newton left Cambridge on September 12 and returned exactly one week later. So private was this reunion that their London friends were unaware that it had even taken place. The mathematician David Gregory, with whom Newton had recently visited in the city, wrote to inform him that "Mr. Fatio hath been in the country some days"—this three weeks after the secret meeting.

The renewal of the friendship also led to a revitalized correspondence, although none of the letters exchanged between the time of Fatio's return and November 1692 have come down to us, quite possibly because

they were intentionally destroyed. We do know that Fatio
visited Cambridge and was shown some of Newton's
most advanced mathematical papers. After informing
Huygens that he was "frozen stiff" by the incomparable
experience, he paid at least one other visit to Newton's
chambers at some point in the late autumn of 1692.
Fatio drafted a chilling follow-up letter on November 17
that shook Newton to his very foundations.

> I have Sir allmost no hopes of seeing you again. With
> coming from Cambridge I got such a grevious cold, which
> has fallen upon my lungs. . . . I thank God my soul is
> extremely quiet, in which you have had the chief hand.
> My head is something out of order, and I suspect I will
> grow worse and worse. The Imperial powders, of which I
> have taken today four of the weakest sort, and one of the
> best sort, have proved quite unsignificant. . . . Were I in a
> lesser feaver I should tell You sir many things. If I am to
> depart this life I could wish my eldest brother, a man of
> extraordinary integrity, could succeed me in your friend-
> ship. As yet I have no Doctor.[12]

Fatio's offer of his brother's friendship in place of
his own has been compared by Newton's psychoanalytic
biographer, Frank Manuel, to the last desperate act of a
dying woman: In choosing a successor for her husband
she proves her love and eliminates a series of potential
rivals.[13] But if Fatio feared that he was truly dying, why
had he not called in a physician? More plausibly, it
appears to have been a melodramatic attempt to assure
himself that the genius of the age cared for him above
all others. If indeed this was Fatio's hope, it was quickly
realized. Newton's hastily drafted reply summoned up
a pathos unlike any he had ever expressed:

> I . . . last night received your letter with wch how much I
> was affected I cannot express. Pray procure ye advice &
> Assistance of Physitians before it bee too late & if you

want any money I will supply you. I rely upon ye character you give of your elder brother & if I find yt my acquaintance may be to his advantage I intend he shall have it, & I hope yt you may still live to bring it about, but for fear of ye worst let me know how I may send a letter &, if need be, a parcel to him.[14]

It had taken three days for Fatio's letter to reach Cambridge. Newton's reply arrived in London the day after it was written, suggesting that he contracted the services of a special carrier in hopes of outracing death. He need not have bothered. "I hope the worst is over," Fatio wrote on the twenty-second. "My lungs are much better, tho' I have still a cold upon them."[15] The truth is, this temperamental, hypochondriacal soul was blessed with a physical constitution the equal of his prodigious idol's, which he proved by living another sixty-one years.

Events then took what appears to be a critical turn. "I feare ye London air conduces to your indisposition," a still worried Newton wrote on January 24, 1693, "& therefore wish you would remove hither so soon as ye weather will give you leave to take a journey." Fatio replied that he must return to the Continent, for his mother had recently died, leaving him an inheritance. He was intrigued by Newton's offer nonetheless and asked for more particulars: "if You wish I should go there [Cambridge] and have for that some other reasons than what barely relateth to my health and to the saving of charges [living expenses] I am ready to do so; But I could wish in that case You would be plain in your next letter."[16]

Newton responded to Fatio's query by mailing him £14, ostensibly to cover the cost of some inconsequential purchases made during their collaboration on scientific matters. He also commented on the question of living arrangements. "The chamber next to me is disposed of;

but that which I was contriving was, that since your want of health would not give you leave to undertake your design for a subsistence at London, to make you such an allowance as might make your subsistence here easy to you."[17] If Newton had anything else in mind he could not bring himself to put it on paper.

Fatio again flexed his emotional muscle by offering him hope: "I could wish, Sir, to live all my life, or the greatest part of it, with you, if that was possible, and shall always be glad to any such methods to bring that to pass as shall not be chargeable to You and a burthen to Your estate or family." He added that Locke hoped they might join him at Oates in Essex, where the repatriated political philosopher was residing with Lady Masham. Fatio saw himself as the bait in this projected colloquium *à trois*. "Yet I think he means well & would have me go there only that You may be the sooner inclinable to come."[18]

The last of Fatio's surviving letters to Newton, dated May 18, 1693, bears the markings of a manic personality. His inheritance had proved disappointing, but his health was much better, thanks to a generous acquaintance whose secret remedy he had taken with "a wonderful success." Indeed, Fatio himself was now considering medicine as a profession, "which I think would not require above a year or two of my time." He would then go into partnership with the creator of the miraculous new elixir. "I could care for many thousands of people and so make it known in a little while. After which it would be easie to raise a fortune by it." The medicine's only drawback was its emetic quality, but that, he assured Newton, could be overcome without difficulty. Of course, he must expend between £100 and £150 a year "for four years or more before this thing is established. And I dare not propose to any body nor to yourself to be Partners in such a design because of ye many accidents, which could spoil it."[19] Newton must advise him on the proper course, preferably at another private meeting in London.

Still under Fatio's seductive but waning spell, Newton journeyed to the capital two weeks later, and he seems to have made a second trip to London late in June. What passed between the two on these occasions we do not know, except that Fatio abandoned his grandiose design of becoming a wealthy doctor and sadly admitted to Huygens, in September 1694, that he had not heard from his idol for more than seven months.

A biographer of Tuchman's persuasion might reasonably conclude that the Newton-Fatio relationship is deserving of no more than passing mention. After all, their mutual attraction, however powerful, is immaterial to any appraisal of Newton's place in history. Whatever his sexual desires, there is nothing to indicate that they exerted a telling influence on his chosen lifework. Had he been a playwright, artist or novelist, things would be different, for we could then scour his creations for vital clues to the creative impulse, whatever its genesis and form. But science, unlike literature and the arts, is neuter; unchecked emotion becomes its mortal enemy when it is allowed to enter the arena of daily labor. And the fruit of that labor, exhilarating and beautiful though it is, can only be expressed in the most dispassionate symbols known to literate society.

Knowing this, I was still determined to pursue the Fatio question. Bringing a person back to life is not a small thing, as anyone who has attempted it soon realizes. The biographer must reassemble his subject like an intricate mosaic from a vast number of scattered and jumbled pieces. Naturally, I wanted to collect them all, right down to the cells, platelets, and corpuscles. This means that the biographer is necessarily intrusive, "a trespasser even when authorized," as Richard Ellman, the late biographer of James Joyce and Oscar Wilde, observed. He brings an alien point of view to bear, necessarily different from the mixture of self-recrimination and rationalization which his subject has made the centerpiece of his lifelong conversation with himself.[20] The accomplished biographer wishes to know the worst as well as the best, to measure with the same yardstick of candor employed by the novelist while refusing to venture across the boundary separating fact from fiction.

The serious student of Newton soon learns that he is dealing more with a phenomenon than a man. The intellect was too profound, the capacity for rage too great, the desire for seclusion too obsessive. An emotional eunuch, Newton mixed in the world on occasion, but he was never of the world. The whole of his pleasure centered on the isolation he guarded so tenaciously, something within the darkest night of himself that called him home. "There is no Excellent Beauty that hath not some Strangeness in the Proportion," wrote Francis Bacon. And so it was with Newton, for whom some of the human parts were missing. He seems not to have been so much flesh and bone as an abstracted thinking machine, all wheels and gears, like the clockwork universe he created, notwithstanding his insistence that God was no absentee landlord. In the circumstances, Fatio represents a great conundrum.

The solution, Leon Edel would suggest, lies in what he defines as the first principle of the new biography. The writer of a life "must learn to understand man's ways of dreaming, thinking and using his fancy." In other words, the analytic methods pioneered by Freud and refined by his disciples must be applied to the life of one's subject to see through the "rationalizations, the postures, the self-delusions."[21]

It so happens that the distinguished historian Frank E. Manuel has attempted just that. Labeling Fatio "the ape of Newton," Manuel writes that Newton's friendship with the young man became so intense that it broke through in defiance of a puritanical inner censor. "If one adopts Freudian imagery, Newton first identified himself with his mother and took himself as the sexual object; then he found young men resembling himself as he would have had his mother love him. The maternal element in his nature found reinforcement."[22]

To Manuel's credit, his analysis is presented in the form of an hypothesis, and rightly so considering he is forced to rely on murmerings gathered from behind a couch three centuries long. While I, too, am fascinated by Freud and consider him one of the truly original thinkers of our time—a genius if you will—the battle over whether to employ his techniques may be over, but the victory is yet to be sealed. In Newton's case the evidence is not only limited but ambiguous, not least because we know almost nothing of the semiliterate Hannah Newton, who was widowed three months before her son was born. Such analysis, moreover, is involuntary; the person being analyzed has no opportunity to reply. More important still is the fact that psychobiography is highly deterministic, depriving the subject of much of his freedom of action, not to mention the storyteller of his art.

If pressed for a conclusion, I would have to say that it is impossible to be certain how the affections of these alternately ebullient and melancholy men were expressed during their private meetings. There is no question but that Newton's scruples would have raised a formidable barrier to an overt sexual liaison, if, indeed, it ever came to that. On the other hand, the correspondence—with its lavish praise, mutual loneliness at separation, and radical swings of mood—bears haunting overtones of an ill-fated romance. The final rupture, which likely contributed to Newton's mental breakdown of 1693, appears to have been prefigured in their agonizing desire to share the same chambers, a desire quite possibly overshadowed by the fear of what might happen if they were to attempt it. Of this much alone one can be certain: In reaching out to an equally distressed soul, Newton for once proved himself human in the most human of ways.

Yes, the story should be as complete as the evidence will allow, but when the facts are illusive or contradictory, readers must be told. They should be encouraged to peer into the darkened corners of the life to judge for themselves. "Were I in a lesser feaver, I should tell You sir many things." A tantalizing lamentation from across a gulf of centuries.

Whither Fatio?

4

The Biographer and the Widow

During one of a dozen or so readings of *All the Strange Hours*, Loren Eiseley's unorthodox but intriguing autobiography, I scribbled the following query at the end of Chapter Eight: "Where's *Mabel?*" As Eiseley's would-be biographer, I was deeply puzzled by the literary naturalist's failure to so much as mention his wife of nearly forty years. By the time Eiseley finishes his story as a man in his mid-sixties, the former Mabel Langdon, who was once his high school English teacher back in Lincoln, Nebraska, is referred to in passing all of three times, and only once by name. Topped, I mused, only by the unpopular Martin Van Buren and enigmatic Henry Adams, whose "autobiographies" give not the slightest hint that either ever had a wife.

Eiseley claimed that it was Mabel's choice to remain in the background, that it was she who pledged him to silence concerning their marriage. A letter Mabel wrote to a friend in September 1975, some two months before the autobiography appeared in bookstores, seemed to confirm as much:

> Loren is always rather upset when any book of his is released, and this time, because of the personal nature of the material, he is even more anxious. . . . Nor am I more than briefly referred to. This was my wish—I wanted to

have our private life remain private. I do not wish to take
the public too intimately into our personal domain. . . . I
never, of course, dictate in literary matters, but I did
express my feelings, and they were observed.[1]

Though I was yet to see Mabel's letter when I began
my biographical quest in the spring of 1984, I had every
reason to be wary as the time neared to approach the
widow. During a reconnaissance to survey the Eiseley
papers in Philadelphia, James Dallet, then Director of
the University of Pennsylvania Archives, informed me
that Mabel had once requested that the material be
returned to her. When Dallet reminded Mabel that the
gift had been unconditional and that she had received a
healthy tax write-off for her generosity, the matter was
dropped. Moreover, I had read the recently published
account of English Professor E. Fred Carlisle, who had
aspired to become Eiseley's literary biographer. Three
months before his death on July 8, 1977, a cancer-
riddled Eiseley wrote to inform Carlisle that he had
decided to destroy his papers. "I am adamant in my
decision to answer no more questions from anyone."
What Carlisle finally produced in 1983 was a hybrid,
part biography and part literary criticism. When he
asked Mabel what she thought of the work, the widow
replied bluntly that she did not care for it in the least.
"My real error," Carlisle lamented, "occurred when I
assumed that Loren Eiseley *would* at some time reveal
things about his life that he did not carefully control or
stage."[2]

In the months of preliminary research that followed,
I rarely passed a day beyond the range of Mabel's
censorious eye. Yet hoping that her attitude might have
softened over time, I wrote to inform her that I was
soon to spend a sabbatical at Penn working in the
archives and interviewing her husband's colleagues and
friends. At minimum I would like to telephone; that is,

if she didn't mind my using her unlisted number, which had been given to me by an old acquaintance anxious that Mabel's part of the story be told. A meeting, perhaps over lunch, would be better.

Carlisle had at least received a reply, but for all I knew my letter, a photocopy of which I read again and again in a futile search for an offending passage, never reached its destination on the Main Line. A fellow biographer who listened to my tale of woe during lunch one day tried to lift my spirits with a bit of gallows humor: "It would be a lot easier for all of us if only someone would shoot the widow."

I returned to Philadelphia in June, having rented a one-bedroom apartment on the twenty-first floor of Nichols House, a Penn graduate dormitory near the heart of campus. Almost every weekday found me ensconced behind a huge oak table deep within the bowels of Franklin Field, the landmark brick and mortar football stadium that has obviously seen better days. It is here, unbeknownst to all but a few historically-minded aficionados, that the treasures of a great Ivy League university are housed in thousands of acid-free cartons strung along dark and forbidding corridors reminiscent of pharaonic tombs. It took me almost four months to go through every page contained in the forty-two boxes of the Eiseley collection, whose accession numbers still slip in and out of my less pleasurable dreams.

However, it did not take nearly as long to discover that something was amiss. To begin with, the papers included not one scrap of correspondence between Eiseley and the members of his family, including his deaf and widowed mother, Daisy, who remained in Lincoln when her son moved East, and an older half brother named Leo, who died in Phoenix only months before Loren. Also missing were the literary exchanges—to which Eiseley himself occasionally referred in print—

with such fellow luminaries as Lewis Mumford, W. H. Auden, Howard Nemerov, and Ray Bradbury. Nor were the folders containing reviews of Eiseley's sixteen books of poetry and prose any less misleading. They had been purged of all but the encomiums. On the other hand, fan letters were preserved by the score, especially those prophesying such Olympian laurels as the Noble Prize (false prophets as it turned out).

Mabel, as I was about to learn, had held some of the correspondence and certain of the notebooks in reserve, at least partly as a hedge against financial disaster, for the Eiseleys, though childless and economically secure, had been forever scarred by the Great Depression. The widow had also participated in a rite as old as paper itself. "I have a good many snapshots," Mabel wrote long-time friend and author Dorothy Thomas Buicke-rood in September 1980, mostly undated, and not placed in albums, which worry me as I don't know what I should do with them. I don't really want them to fall into strange hands." As for her correspondence with Loren when he was in Philadelphia taking his M.A. and Ph.D. in the mid-1930s:

> I burned all of my precious letters because they are much too personal ever to be read by anyone but me. Even if we leave instructions that certain things be destroyed there is always the terrible possibility that someone will think it 'too bad' to carry out the order. So I take no chances. Loren said, 'I want our private life to remain private.' And so it shall, so far as I have any say about it.[3]

Five years earlier Mabel had indicated that the wish for absolute privacy was hers rather than her husband's. The time was not far off when I would be in a position to judge for myself.

Meanwhile the interviews were going well, with one troubling exception. Whenever the focus shifted from

Eiseley to Mabel, the person reminiscing would inevitably falter. Typical in this regard was Froelich Rainey, the normally loquacious director emeritus of the University Museum. "Fro" and Eiseley were born within months of one another, and both had come to Penn in the autumn of 1947. Anthropologists by training, the two devised and team-taught a popular undergraduate course titled World Archaeology. "We had great fun," Rainey laughingly recalled. "We never got around to writing a syllabus in all the time we taught it," much to the annoyance of certain envious colleagues. Eiseley's delivery reminded Rainey of a Methodist minister: "The words just rolled out; beautiful language and beautiful sentences." But many of their students grew restless, for the staging was simply "too perfect." Nor did Eiseley have any patience with freshmen who tried to "horn in" during their post-lecture discussions. "You have to shut them up," he groused. And when the bell sounded, "Loren went zip out of there just as fast as could be." He, least of anyone, had solutions to the problems and crises dogging civilization in the twentieth century. They would be solved once and for all, he confided to Fro, by the return of the next great ice.

"What about the widow?" I asked.

"Funny thing about Mabel," Rainey mused after a long pause. "On the face of it a kind of recessive character. . . . Then she had a funny side. She'd sit down and rattle off ragtime on the piano, which was so uncharacteristic of what you expected of her."

"And what of the marriage?"

"I think she was entirely wrapped up in Loren; her life was Loren. He was not only husband but children and everything else."[4]

This was about all that a friend of over thirty years had to offer, but it was also more than most of Eiseley's other colleagues could contribute.

By September my scheduled departure from Philadelphia was less than two weeks away when the telephone rang early one evening. The caller was Mary Crooks, Eiseley's one-time secretary during his brief and misguided stint as provost of Penn. Mary, a resident of the same Wynnewood apartment complex as Mrs. Eiseley, had informed Mabel that she was going to show me about the grounds, prompting the widow to ask that Mary bring me by for a short visit. When the phone rang again two days later, my spirits plummeted. It was Mary Crooks, doubtless about to deliver the not unexpected coup de grace. But instead of cancelling the visit, Mabel had invited us to lunch, with the understanding that she wanted to speak privately with me afterward. The adrenalin began pulsing twice as fast as before, yet my elation was tinged with a certain foreboding. A private audience. Was a man in his early forties about to receive a severe dressing down from a tough-minded octogenarian?

Mary Crooks, a tall, white-haired spinster with the affecting glow of her Irish forebears, met me at the depot around ten o'clock. We walked the two blocks to her apartment in the Wyndon, a comfortable but architecturally undistinguished complex within a stone's throw of a bustling shopping center on City Avenue. Most convenient for running errands, I thought to myself, but hardly the domestic setting one would expect of the gifted nature writer who penned such classic essays as "The Star Thrower," "The Flow of the River," and "How Flowers Changed the World." Mary talked a bit about Mabel, of her frailty and unwillingness to socialize with old friends. With the exception of regular visits to the doctor, she rarely set foot outside her door. Nor would she purchase a television set to watch the concerts and theater she so loved, thus keeping faith with a husband who argued that such a "machine"

(Eiseley's quaint appellation for all things electrical, including computers) would surely alienate the muse.

At exactly 11:45, we walked down two flights of stairs and knocked on Mabel's door. It was opened by Mary Smith, the Eiseley's long-time housekeeper and occasional cook, who commuted twice a week from West Philadelphia. She asked us to make ourselves comfortable; Mabel was running a little late.

I took a seat on a long sofa opposite a huge oil painting of giant sunflowers, a poignant reminder of Eiseley's nostalgia for the sunflower forests of his youth. Before me, on the maple coffee table, lay several volumes authored by fellow Nebraskan Wright Morris, Eiseley's boon companion of many years. Compulsive bibliophiles, the two had roamed the city's used bookstores with a passion put to use, returning home soiled from "toe to topknot" at the end of the day, the circulation in their fingers cut off by the heavy cord binding their unwieldy treasure. Early in their relationship, Morris nicknamed his melancholy friend "Schmerzie," short for *Weltschmerz* (world pain). Stealing over to Morris's apartment whenever he could, Eiseley once confessed to the pleasure he took when the two harangued each other on the foul state of the world. In a corner of the living room stood Mabel's walnut spinet. I tiptoed over to steal a peek at the yellowing sheet music—Scott Joplin's "Maple Leaf Rag."

Moments later, the outline of a slowly moving shadow appeared on the wall. I rose to my feet, wholly unprepared for the specter about to enter the room. Mabel emerged, and every aspect of her appearance conformed to the vision of old age projected in "Twilight Musing," a poem she had published over half a century earlier in the *Prairie Schooner*, the little magazine where Eiseley had also gotten his start. Elegant with a patrician bearing, Mabel indeed wore her pure white hair waved and low-knotted by a ribbon at the neck. As she had predicted, her hands remained soft and lovely through the years. And who could doubt that Mabel took her rest on covers of silk, a living creation of her own memory:

> *So deep in sleep that I shall never know—*
> *Girl with brown hair and youth so dear to her—*
> *If you stand quietly without my door*
> *And whisper of your love and pity me.*

The only things missing were tapers in their silver candlesticks for casting "shadows dancing on the walls."[5]

I walked across the room and clasped the delicate hand she offered. Her deep gray eyes never once left mine, nor would she release my hand. Tears began to well, and for the first time I knew exactly how Pip felt when he was brought into the company of Miss Havisham. Finally, I was the one who flinched by motioning toward an overstuffed chair that Mary Smith had singled out as Mabel's favorite.

My attempt at small talk proved a disaster. Mabel was not the least bit interested in the weather, and she acknowledged my remarks with an economy of words bordering on disdain. I was much relieved when lunch was served a few minutes later, but the tension began rebuilding as the time neared for our tete-a-tete. Mary Crooks soon excused herself, leaving biographer and widow face to face in what seemed at the time the loneliest place in the cosmos.

Without forewarning, Mabel looked me dead in the eye with a glare worthy of Torquemada and exclaimed, "Well, what did you get out of Joe Fraser?" Her intelligence, like that of the Spanish Grand Inquisitor, was superb, for my visit with the retired Director of the Pennsylvania Academy of the Fine Arts had only taken place the day before. Mabel, who had gone to work as registrar of the Academy in 1952, was promoted to assistant director three years later, a position she held until her retirement in 1969.

I somehow knew that if I flinched at this early stage of the game, all would be lost. Returning Mabel's stare, I deadpanned: "Joe Fraser told me you were his right-hand *man*." The eyes softened, the mouth began to curl upward, and Mabel broke into laughter for the first time. Olé!

She then took a deep breath, and said, "Well, tell me what you want to know."

Affecting nonchalance, I reached into the briefcase at my feet, bypassing the little recording machine for which Loren Eiseley nurtured a deep aversion. Instead, I withdrew a yellow legal pad and pen, then crossed the room and seated myself in front of Mabel on a dining room chair. Glancing at the thin band of silver on her left hand, I started by asking her about their meeting and early courtship, which eventually led to an engagement lasting eleven years.

Thus began a remarkably intimate conversation that was to last more than two hours. Mabel's memory was as acute as that of any of the twenty or so professors I had already interviewed, perhaps because she still inhabited a world that ended for everyone else when her husband succumbed in a stark hospital room seven years before. While the widow occasionally faltered, she never once flinched. Each time the tears came, I either gave her a moment to compose herself or gently changed the subject, feeling all the while like one guilty of a crime beyond articulation, a felony compounded by my inability to desist.

I was well aware that Eiseley had been discontent with his personal history and that he had invented another which, however fictitious, enabled him to operate in the real world. Skillful projections of the self, much of his "autobiographical" writing constitutes a series of masks. Pain, beautifully rendered pain, became his leitmotif, the narrative shrouded in that ineffable melancholy the Spanish call *triste*. Above all, he attempted to create the myth of the self-sufficient loner who, like Thoreau, with whom he is often compared as a writer, created the grand illusion that the forest and the badlands were his natural abode.

"Every word Loren wrote was true," Mabel asserted, striking the arm of her chair with a gnarled fist for emphasis. Yet nearly everything she told me of her husband and their relationship seemed to contradict this dubious claim. Far from the solitary loner who occupied most of the poetry and prose, Eiseley was the type of person who needed constant reassurance lest he dissolve altogether into the elements, a man willing to allow others to do what he could not or would not do for himself. It was Mabel, seven years his senior, who had taken the drifting, adolescent Loren in tow, she who had provided him with money and saw to it that he returned to the University of Nebraska after dropping out several times, she who—in her own words—had "submerged her ambitions to become a writer" for his sake. As Rudolph Umland, Eiseley's old friend and editor during their depression days with the Nebraska Writers' Project, sagely observed, "It was Mabel who made a famous man out of him."[6]

When the interview was over, Mabel leaned back and let slip a sigh of regret: "You know, I've done something that my husband probably wouldn't have approved of." Then she smiled and added, "I was going to be very aloof today, and just look what I've told you."

The final tears came at the moment of my departure, but this time they were not Mabel's alone, for we both knew that this would be our one and only meeting.

She promised, however, that I could use her private number in the future, and the interviews continued by telephone until she became bedridden a year later, too ill to speak with anyone at length. She also promised me access to the correspondence and notebooks still in her possession, a pledge honored by her sister and heir.

Mabel died in her sleep on the night of July 28, 1986, having turned eighty-six three weeks earlier. I debated whether to fly East for the funeral, but finally decided not to go on the grounds that my motives might appear suspect to relatives and close friends, a decision I have regretted ever since. I did, however, telephone the news to a few of the old-timers who had aided me during my research, a small gesture of tribute that resulted in a fleeting but strangely comforting sense of family.

Mabel was buried next to her "Larry" beneath a roughhewn stone bearing an inscription from one of Eiseley's poems: "We loved the world but could not stay."[7] Had she chosen to have a monument of her own, I can think of no more fitting epitaph than these lines from Tennyson's "Daydream,"

> *And o'er the hills, and far away*
> *Beyond their utmost purple rim,*
> *Beyond the night, across the day,*
> *Through all the world she followed him.*

5

The Lady of the Masque

One autumn day not so very long ago, a sharp-eyed citizen of Lincoln, Nebraska, happened to be browsing the shelves of a local used bookstore. She chanced to open an aging volume of childrens' stories and there on the flyleaf was the following inscription, obviously in a child's hand:

Loren Corey Eiseley
1811 South Street
Lincoln, Nebraska

A thorough search of the shelves yielded another dozen or so similarly inscribed volumes. All were purchased for the price of a few dollars, then dutifully carted off to Lincoln's Bennett Martin Public Library for deposit in the Heritage Room, along with certain documents and memorabilia of other highly acclaimed Nebraska authors such as Willa Cather, John G. Neihardt, and Mari Sandoz.

Without realizing it, this unsung bibliophile had performed a considerable service on behalf of Eiseley's future biographer. Eiseley once stated that his parents were too poor to buy him books, an assertion belied by his signature in the classics *Robinson Crusoe, From the Earth to the Moon, Black Beauty, Treasure Island,* and *Before Adam.* Yet this was but the beginning of a bizarre and unsettling tale whose ending is worthy of William Syd-

ney Porter, whom Eiseley's generation knew and admired as O. Henry.

At the bottom of the box containing Eiseley's childhood books was a much different sort of volume, one
Alexander Johnson's *Ten—and Out! The Complete Story of
the Prize Ring in America*. Published in 1927 when Eiseley
was a young man of twenty, it too bore his inscription
and the address of his uncle, William Buchanan Price,
an attorney who, together with Loren's aunt Grace, had
taken the youth and Grace's widowed sister in following
the death of Loren's father, a desperate Willy Loman
figure who lived life on the rim between reality and
imagination. By this time Eiseley was an undergraduate
at the University of Nebraska, writing poetry and an
occasional short story for the *Prairie Schooner*, one of the
many so-called "little mags" that proliferated on the eve
of the Great Depression.

Eiseley was frequently seen in the company of the
Schooner's editor, Lowry Charles Wimberly, an insub-
stantial figure who trudged the streets of Lincoln in a
dark, ill-fitting overcoat and Confederate-style slouch
hat, his sallow countenance turned into the wind. Allegedly true accounts of death by violent means, the gorier
the better, fascinated the inscrutable English professor.
Wimberly purchased almost every issue of *True Detective*,
Master Detective, *Inside Detective*, and *Startling Detective*
and conjectured that if Shakespeare, Browning, and De
Quincey were alive they too would be reading crime
magazines.

The "Doc," as he was affectionately known to an
adoring circle of aspiring Jack Londons, was forced to
settle for a form of controlled mayhem on Saturday
nights. Accompanied by Eiseley, he attended illegal
boxing matches, betting a dollar or two on the outcome
of each bout. "They were the shabby little back street
affairs of the depression," Eiseley recalled, "generally

held in some local garage or something of that kind."[1]
Men drank illegal hooch from amber-necked bottles
secreted in brown paper, puffed furiously on cheap
cigars, and turned vulgar when their favorite gladiator
hit the blood-spattered floor and failed to rise. For some
reason, Wimberly liked to go about town in threes. Thus
Eiseley and the Doc were often joined by Preston
Holder, a physically rugged youth who rode the hurtling freights with panache and extolled the virtues of
the classic boxing lithographs by George Bellows.

When the time came to accession the volume on
prizefighting, fate took a hand in a manner rarely even
dreamt about by the biographer. The rough, partially
missing, draft of an old letter fluttered to the floor, as if
in counterpoint to the somber message it contained. It
was written to a woman identified only as Lila. Beyond
this, the letter contained no address, no date, and few
clues. Only two things were certain: the writing was
Loren Eiseley's and its author had set forth a wrenching
cri de coeur.

It seems that he had heard nothing from Lila for
several months, and was growing more anxious by the
day. Hoping to pierce this vacuum of silence, he had
written an earlier letter, asking if anything were the
matter. Lila finally replied, dealing him a telling blow.
She had married a "Mr. Graves" the previous autumn.
Loren responded in turn, and it is the draft of this letter
that survives.

Though no one had ever seen Eiseley so much as
put on a boxing glove, he created the illusion—doubtless inspired by his weekend outings with Wimberly and
Holder—that he had taken several beatings in the ring
of late, but nothing to compare with this withering
assault on his emotions. Even worse, he was supposedly
bedridden when Lila's announcement arrived. Still, he
lamely agreed that they should remain friends in spite

of what had happened, and even promised to pay her a visit:

Your letter arrived when I was very ill with influenzal heart neurosis—hence my belated (and very envious!) congratulations. You're a real sport Lila, I'm going to take advantage of your invitation. Though first I've got to get well—I'm a very scrawny sight at present and don't know whether I'll ever be able to put on a glove again. Oh well, there are compensations, if not I'll be quitting while my nose is still in its usual prominent position. But I'm coming, yes indeed.

Late last autumn—maybe about the time you were married—I went on a picnic with some friends down to a secluded spot in the hill country near Weeping Water—which if you've been down there you'll remember as one of the loveliest spots in this rather uninteresting State. I had taken a nice lacing from a fast man a day before and was properly bruised up and disgruntled. It was growing dusk when I and a friend went back up the winding road through the hills to get some dishes from the car. I walked wearily along nursing a battered eye when suddenly the utter silence of the place aroused me.

. . . At that moment, Lila, I saw you for one ecstatic instant clothed in a white dress walking toward me in the twilight down that hill.

I stopped and gasped so audibly that Shorty asked me what was wrong.

Do you understand, Lila? I don't think for a moment there was anything supernatural about it. The place and hour . . . combined with my overstrung mood made me the momentary victim of an hallucination I suppose. But that is a little of what I think of you. And there is no beautiful thing that doesn't make me lonely for your presence.

I have read a few books—I have called myself a realist—I have no philosophy except the belief that the universe is indifferent and blind. And so believing why has one voice—your voice—and a few brief memories weight enough to drive me restless out of class rooms to the waste land and the high white solitude of autumn stars? Why should I who believe that at the moment of my death I am as utterly obliterated as the torn leaf or the crushed ant be troubled by something out of reach when the years are passing and there is so much that is 'sensible' to be attained and enjoyed?

What is it you psychologists would call it, a 'fixation,' a 'monomania' or something?

. . . I have been something of a failure I expect— I have taken more beatings—physical and mental— than are respectable for any man and yet I think perhaps after all I am very lucky—and I know that I am proud.

To have loved something fine and high and lovely enough to make oneself forever unsatisfied and driven is a satisfaction even when one stumbles and fails.

I have that pride and the sweet fine gesture of your letter made sure it would remain.

So you see I shant need to shatter my last illusion. If anything it is reborn. The fact that someone else is a lucky man alters nothing in my attitude. It makes you forever remote and unattainable, but it doesn't stop me from loving you. That's impossible. You will always be the ghost in the dusk on the road to Weeping Water, the suntanned little lady who was to tell me about silence up on the Navajo.

And you may expect me at the unexpected time.

Loren[2]

As a romantic gesture, I privately christened the missive the "Lila letter," after the fictional Yuri Zhivago's bittersweet correspondence with the beautiful Lara. Although the document was shown to me in October 1984, the mystery surrounding both recipient and sender would not be solved until January 1986 when, after more than a year of intensive but fruitless inquiry, I decided to make one last attempt before filing it away forever.

From beginning to end, my quest hinged on a single passage: "What is it you psychologists call it, a 'fixation,' a 'monomania' or something?" Whatever else she might have been, Lila was almost certainly a woman of some education. Based on my knowledge of Eiseley's early handwriting and the publication date of Johnson's history of boxing—1927—I began collecting the names of every Lila enrolled at the University of Nebraska during the last three years of the decade. Since class lists were either incomplete or nonexistent, I did much of the research at Love Library, the repository of every edition of the *Cornhusker*, Nebraska's prosaically titled yearbook. It was a painstaking process that yielded some fifteen names in all, yet a list that I suspected was far from complete. (Had "my" Lila quit the university to wed?)

Armed with this data, I introduced myself to one of the gracious ladies staffing the Alumni Office, who cheerfully humored an eccentric but apparently harmless visiting professor. It turned out that some of my candidates had never registered with the alumni association while others had passed away many years earlier. Seven long-distance calls to those remaining on the list yielded a curious mixture of surprise, laughter and, most of all, sympathy, but no Lila who had known Loren Eiseley—or at least none who would admit that she had.

Since the groom's name was Graves, I also requested that the files be checked for all males with this surname, which had taken on metaphorical overtones given the moribund state of my research. Another blank. Nor did I fare any better with those who had known Eiseley in his high school and undergraduate days. The many interviews I conducted during the intervening months produced not one hint as to Lila's identity. Somewhat sheepishly, I even asked Eiseley's widow if the name meant anything to her, but not before soliciting the other information I required as insurance against banishment. "No," Mabel replied in an even voice, "I don't recall knowing anyone by that name."[3]

The day finally arrived when I began to question the authenticity of the letter itself. Perhaps Eiseley had written it as part of a class exercise. Lowry Wimberly, who served as both editor and mentor to the young writer, surely would have relished the sentiment. Wimberly found it difficult to reject a well-written piece concerned with telepathy, precognition or any other branch of parapsychology. His own *Schooner* stories, "Dispossessed" and "The Red Gentian," were based on certain of these very themes. Later on, Eiseley himself purchased many works on the paranormal, especially those representing the more scholarly English school.

The Lila letter, which had been set aside for lack of progress, resurfaced at the point where I was preparing to write of Eiseley's early manhood. By this time I knew that he had fallen in love with and eventually married his student teacher, a woman seven years his senior. Could Lila have been an "older woman?" I wondered. In the letter she speaks of the day "when we are all grown old and respectable," a day when he can call upon her "without exciting the neighbors' comment!"

The female voice on the other end of the line seemed dubious. The new computer system was not fully operational as yet, but she would do her best. If I could leave my number she would get back to me in a week or so. Yes, my instructions were clear. She would run the name Lila Graves for each graduating class beginning with 1923, the year Eiseley entered Teachers College High School on the university campus.

Two days later the mists parted. The Lila Graves I had been seeking was once Lila Fern Wyman. She had graduated from Nebraska in the spring of 1924, with a bachelor's degree in education. Lila was no longer living, but her file contained the names and addresses of a niece and nephew. With their cooperation and a bit of additional research during yet another visit to Lincoln, I was able to piece together as much of the story as one would ever know.

Born on August 5, 1902 at Walnut, a village in western Iowa near Council Bluffs, Lila was the next-to-youngest daughter of Burton A. and Letitia Flood Wyman. Her grandfather, A.B. Wyman, was a successful farmer and politician who also owned a lucrative transportation business. No bridge spanned the Missouri River between Council Bluffs and Omaha before 1872. There was, however, a ferry that accommodated horse-drawn wagons. A.B. Wyman owned several drays and omnibuses, which were used to haul freight and passengers brought west by rail over to the Nebraska side of the river. When A.B. died, he left his considerable estate to Burton's children, with the proviso that their father serve as trustee.

The large family, which also included two boys, moved frequently, for Burton, a severe asthmatic, was ever in search of a more beneficial climate. He preferred small towns and always sought out the largest residence available. Letitia left virtually all of the domestic duties to her seven daughters or family servants, preferring to occupy her time making buttonholes and playing chess. Indeed, she vowed that none of her girls would ever marry a man ignorant of the finer points of what she considered the world's most challenging game, one which, incidentally, Eiseley never played. When the daughters began to reach college age, Burton moved his family into a rambling frame home at 2620 R Street in Lincoln. Here Letitia indulged her fashion-conscious progeny by hiring a foreign girl to sew for them full time.

Having distinguished herself in the classroom, Lila, along with twelve of her peers, was initiated into the prestigious Order of the Black Masque, the university chapter of Mortar Board, a national senior honor society for women. Facial coverings in place, their hands ostentatiously secluded in the loose-fitting sleeves of their academic gowns, the thirteen coeds posed for their official picture, which appeared in the 1924 *Cornhusker*.

Lila was also a member of the sorority Chi Delta Phi, the Palladian Literary Society, the Y.M.C.A. Cabinet, and Theta Sigma Phi, an intercollegiate journalism fraternity. In a group photograph of the latter organization, the mask and academic regalia have been removed to reveal a dark-haired, dark-eyed sensuous charmer, an effect heightened by the fact that, in contrast to the prim, high-necked blouses worn by the other young women, Lila chose the open-collared chemise of a flapper.

When she was ready to begin student teaching in September 1923, Lila, or Miss Wyman as she was known to her pupils, was assigned to Teachers College High School, where she was put in charge of English V. It was here that Loren Eiseley, a junior five years younger than she, encountered the first woman who truly stirred his heart. It was for her that he composed an emotional essay about his fictional dog Whiskers, who was supposedly killed by a neighbor's pack of hounds. He would save the tepid praise Miss Wyman scribbled at the bottom for over fifty years: "I like the informal air of this."[4]

His semester mark of 92 in English V was exceeded only by sterling 96s in medieval history and botany.

Eiseley's teasing classmates obviously knew whereof they spoke when they drafted the class will: "Loren Eiseley bequests his ability to Carl Meyer, provided he does not vamp the teachers." By this time the lady of the mask had been succeeded by the elegant and prim Miss Mabel Langdon, Eiseley's senior English student teacher whom he would marry thirteen years later.

The Wymans' unusual graduation present seems to have been a perfect choice for Lila, the most free-spirited of their seven daughters. In the summer of 1924 she embarked on a passage to India to visit her older sister and brother-in-law, medical missionaries who were living in the Tamil-speaking city of Madurai at the southernmost tip of the subcontinent. According to her niece and nephew, their aunt fell in love with some unknown man while sailing the Pacific. He jilted her, and the resulting emotional trauma was so great that she was institutionalized in California after her return. It was probably there that she met the handsome, soft-spoken Robert Graves, a hotel manager whom she married on the rebound, in 1926. Eiseley apparently saw little, if anything, of his first love after this, and he soon began to focus his attentions on Mabel.

In the end, Lila's marriage—like that of Dante's beloved Beatrice—elevated her to the position of an icon in Loren's eyes, and he doubtless never learned of the tragedy that marred the life of his madonna in white. The Graves' only child, a two-year-old son named Bobby, was running about the yard one day in June 1930, while his mother hung out the family wash. Some neighbor boys came along and began playing on the cistern cover at the side of the house. Somehow, they managed to drag the heavy concrete object aside, and Bobby fell to his death in the dark waters below. Lila and Robert divorced not long thereafter, and she attended the University of Chicago as a graduate student in sociology. She later moved to New Orleans, where she was employed by the state as a social worker. Lila never remarried and, like a character from the pen of Tennessee Williams, lived the rest of her life in quiet obscurity with a female companion. She died of heart failure in 1974, at age seventy-two, in the Louisiana town of Natchitoches, famous for its moss-bearded live oaks and gracious antebellum mansions. Her remains were cremated and the ashes sent north for burial in the family plot in Walnut Hill Cemetery at Council Bluffs on the Missouri.

I gave myself high marks for the perseverance that led to the solution of this biographical mystery, but it saddened me to learn the rest of the story—and not only because of its tragic outcome. Once the facts were known, I could no longer daydream, as Eiseley must have through the years, of the various fortunes that might have befallen the woman who had rent a fragile heart.

Way leads on to way, and Lila was far from my thoughts when, one afternoon, a line in a photocopied letter from the Eiseley estate caused me to reflect on the tragedy once more. My reverie was suddenly interrupted by the telephone and an operator asking if I would accept a collect call from a woman in Louisiana. The name rang no bell, so I politely refused. Luckily, the caller was persistent. In a heavy southern drawl she identified herself as Mrs. Eloise Stephens from Natchitoches, a relative of the woman with whom Lila had lived for many years and whose existence had been made known to me by Lila's nephew. We had talked only once a year and a half earlier, and then but briefly. Mrs. Stephens had recently been going through some old cartons and had discovered a few items that once belonged to Lila. They were already packed and on their way to me via parcel post.

Within a day or two I was reading from Lila's almost empty diary, dated 1924:

July 13: Left my dear family and Ernest—start to India.

July 16: Had 45 min. sight-seeing trip in Salt Lake City. Hot dusty ride thru desert all afternoon.

July 17: Passports all finished.

July 18: Visit Berkeley campus A.M. with Marian and Paul B. Saw Clara Wilson. Drive with Ethel & Walter to Palo Alto to Leland Stanford's and their house for dinner.

July 19: Aboard *Pres. Polk*! Much thrilled—Beautiful boat! 7 pds. candy—3 doz. red roses—beautiful basket flowers—Mrs. Wilson saw me off.

July 20: Yes! seasick! but not very: sea very rough. Ate three meals in cabin. Terrible blue and homesick.

July 26: Beautiful on ocean. Walked deck all A.M. with Mrs. Owen. Played bridge & tea with Mrs. Brady, Captain. Read some letters.

There were to be no further entries, no word on whether any of the letters were from Eiseley.

The box also contained at least a dozen enlarged photographs of Lila's baby, as well as a book with a pink cover detailing the infant's progress. Bobby's first gifts were a white gold ring and a blue rattle, both bestowed by his father and namesake. He had first smiled at 36 hours of age, first laughed at four months, and cut his first tooth at seven months, adding four more by his first birthday, which was celebrated with a five-layer cake decorated with caramel frosting topped by a single white candle.

I had seen and read enough, too much in fact, and was preparing to place the forlorn contents back in their carton when a small lump, barely visible in the wadded packing at the bottom, caught my eye. I reached in and pulled out a discolored sack; inside, with their delicate bindings still fastened, were a crinkled pair of the lost baby's shoes.

6

"Old RU" and "The Gaff"

Working, as he usually does, at a polished table in the weighty silence of an archive, the contemporary historian has a tendency to forget that his profession is rooted in what Carl Becker termed that ancient and honorable company of wise men of the tribe—of gregarious bards and storytellers and wandering minstrels, of soothsayers and priests and epic poets to whom was entrusted the collective wisdom, both human and divine. This is especially so when, as in my case, the historical quest has concerned those who made their exit centuries past and of whom little survives beyond the written word.

But to the biographer of a more contemporary figure, primary sources comprise more than words and images captured on paper; they are the roof under which one's subject was born, the schoolhouse where he learned his ABCs, the neighborhood streets where he walked hand in hand with his high school sweetheart, and, if one is very lucky, the living memories of those who grew up with him and took his measure, as the cliché goes, "way back when."

Having decided to depart the seventeenth century for the twentieth, I was confronted with the need to employ oral history for the first time. My reading on the subject had been scattershot at best, consisting of such classics as Theodore Rosengarten's *All God's Dangers:*

The Life of Nate Shaw and Ronald Blythe's *Akenfield:*
Portrait of an English Village. These I read for pleasure
rather than for pointers on technique; indeed, the only
tape recorder I owned was an unwieldy reel-to-reel
dinosaur that my father, a one-time salesman of electronic parts, gave to me after exceeding his annual
quota of vacuum tubes, a far cry from the trip to Florida
of which he dreamed.

Loren Eiseley died in July 1977, two months before
his seventieth birthday. This meant that I would be
testing the memories of people who had known him
over half a century earlier, during his high school and
college days in Lincoln, Nebraska—men and women
who grew up in a world of flowered china, oriental
brick-a-brack, and gas-lit parlors only a tick of the clock
removed from Thomas Beer's mauve decade. Doubly
worrisome to me was the fact that Eiseley, a scientist by
training if not by temperament, had never come to grips
with modern technology. When he wanted to make a
phone call, the number was dialed for him by his wife;
like his mentor, the great anthropologist Frank Speck,
he refused to purchase a television set; he owned no
automobile; and the mere thought of the computer was
enough to provoke an eloquent soliloquy on the potential for electronic spying. Approach him with a tape
recorder or bring one to a lecture he was giving and
you risked public censure. It was with such thoughts
that I merged onto Interstate 70 for the six-hundred-
mile drive west to Lincoln in the spring of 1984, the
letters granting me permission to approach my living
archives on the seat beside me. Yet the question in my
mind was this: Would they speak?
Twenty-four hours later found me staring into the
most arresting pair of gray eyes I have ever seen. Almost
transparent, they were wreathed by billows of white hair

and a matching beard, between which a pipe, blackened from years of hard use, projected from the corner of a small but resolute mouth. There was no doubt about it; I was staring into the visage of a clipper ship captain who had somehow slipped through a time warp, only to be cast up on one of the most landlocked shores known to humankind.

Wilbur Gaffney or "Bill" or "The Gaff," as I would come to know him, met me at the door of his ranch house on Lincoln's south side and led me out back to what he affectionately but dubiously called "the garden." Although I am no more than average height, he barely reached my shoulder and moved with a shuffling gait so pronounced he confessed to never walking more than the fifty or so steps to the mail box at the front curb. We seated ourselves in cast iron lawn chairs bearing the signatures of many birds and were soon joined by two jet-black cats, which entertained themselves the afternoon long by cutting figure eights between our legs, a traumatic experience for one whose only interest in felines is to keep them as far away as possible. To our backs, in a tangle of vines, chesthigh weeds, and dying evergreens, could be heard the rustling of squirrels and chipmunks, as well as the occasional hoot of a forlorn owl whose biological clock had somehow taken a wrong turn. Overhead, like a pesky mosquito, droned the engine of a small plane practicing approaches at a nearby airfield. The new battery-operated tape recorder I placed between us on a backless kitchen chair was about to undergo its first and stiffest test.

Gaffney began by recounting the story of how he joined the editorial staff of the University of Nebraska's literary quarterly the *Prairie Schooner*, in 1927. It was here that he met Loren Eiseley, "who was not a proper southsider but a working man's son. That gave us a certain amount of kinship." The two were soon taking

long walks together across the salt flats and gently
rolling countryside surrounding their native Lincoln.
Their standard fare on these expeditions was a bar of
German chocolate—nourishing but not so sweet as to
arouse thirst. Near the bucolic village of Denton to the
southwest, they crossed three or four miles of unfenced
land, which the two fancied was the closest thing to
moors they might ever see. The English and Irish poets
came automatically to mind; they quoted stanzas by
Tennyson, Coleridge, Wordsworth, and Yeats from
memory.

Gaffney remembered the exact spot where they
once paused while Eiseley introduced him to G.K. Chesterton's *The Ballad of the White Horse*, reciting a haunting
stanza on the invasion of England by the Norsemen with
their Christless chivalry:

> *And men brake out of the northern lands,*
> *Enormous lands alone,*
> *Where a spell is laid upon life and lust*
> *And the rain is changed to a silver dust*
> *And the sea to a great green stone.*

Gaffney was so moved that he later committed much of
Chesterton to memory, including all of the beautiful
"Lepanto," which he quoted to an appreciative Eiseley
in return. More remarkable was the fact that Gaffney,
who later joined the English Department at the University of Nebraska, began writing his own epic poem,
which, at the time of the interview, was still unfinished.
I winced when he gestured nonchalantly toward the
house and confided that more than 100,000 lines lay
scattered about the recently flooded basement, "some
very good, others quite bad." Sadly, there were no
children to leave them to.

While they agreed on many things, the two friends

sometimes differed in their opinions about the new generation of poets. Whereas Gaffney was tepid when it came to the works of Robinson Jeffers, Eiseley was enthusiastic about the alienated master of Tor House— the personification of twentieth-century man who knew too much. Eiseley was especially drawn to Jeffers's short poems, but he also read the longer narrative works, which deal with murder, incest, and other kinds of violence. Gaffney remembered him reciting "To the Stone-Cutters," men who fight time with marble, "foredefeated challengers of oblivion." So strong was Jeffers's undertow that it later carried Eiseley all the way to California, where the normally reserved young man wrangled an introduction to the poet via the noted photographer Edward Weston.

One day, when the fledgling writers were in the office of *Schooner* editor Professor Lowry Charles Wimberly, an Edgar Allan Poe lookalike, the "Doc" mused, "Why shouldn't the West have its own 'Graveyard School of Poetry?' Lord knows death was a constant in pioneer days." Needing no further encouragement, the two set about composing several such poems in an attempt to revive the old genre, one or two of which appeared in the early issues of the *Schooner*. Little came of this. Unlike the English poets, Gaffney reminisced, "we didn't have a pious, or overpious . . . sense of a Day of Doom. Also, British churchyards, with yew trees, are perhaps more potentially 'poetic' than bare little graveyards on the brown prairie hills."

Gaffney and his friend always carried notebooks in their shirt pockets in case their muse should chance to pay a call. At times these blank pages were put to less exalted use. They would sit down on the banks of a pond or stream and fashion little paper boats, as they had done when they were schoolboys. The two especially loved the north side of Capital Beach Lake, located on a salt flat. They walked the gently sweeping arc of rimed shore, occasionally bumping shoulders, Eiseley pointing out flora and fauna that Gaffney "wouldn't have begun to recognize." The prevailing summer wind blew salt spray into their deeply tanned faces, while an inland species of gull darted and cried in the distance. Short man and tall, light of foot and heavy turned homeward reluctantly, Tennyson's lines of poetry wafting on the freshening breeze:

In the afternoon they came into a land
In which it seemed always afternoon.

I knew I was in business when, two hours later, the forgotten recorder clicked off automatically, signalling the end of the tape. It was just as well, for by this time Gaffney's soft voice had dropped to whisper, as if in deference to a delicate web of memory too easily disturbed. (Later on, when the time came to transcribe the interview, the poor audio quality gave me fits, not to mention the birds chirping merrily away in the background.) No matter. The Gaff had taught me the most important lesson of interviewing the first time out. So excellent was his recall that I stopped worrying about the extensive list of questions I had planned to ask and listened instead.

As with Gaffney, I had been corresponding with "Old RU," as he occasionally signed his letters, for some time before we met. So far as I know, it has been my only communication with a dead man.

One day, in 1953, while seated at the counter of a cafe in Sargent, Nebraska, Rudolph Umland dropped dead. By his doctor's calculations, he remained so for more than three minutes before his heart was coaxed into pumping again. Umland was not quite the same person afterward. He experienced a continuing "strangeness" that he could not put his finger on and gave cold comfort to friends hoping to catch a vicarious glimpse of eternity. When asked what death was like, Umland replied, "Nothing!" Incredulous, they made him repeat himself. "NOTHING! There was the same oblivion when I lay dead that existed before I was born."[1]

Thirteen years later, Umland collapsed a second time at work, and lay in a coma for two hours. His hair whitened; his stocky frame shrunk until he needed a cane to get about on once powerful legs that wobbled like unbaked pretzels. He was fifty-eight but he had the self-described appearance of a man of seventy-five. By the time we met he had long since retired from the civil service and returned, with his wife Elsie, to Lincoln, where they were living in a spanking new town house on a street called Winding Way. Umland had recovered some of his youthful robustness; his patriarchal beard and complementary mane sparked a vision of the Creator painted on the ceiling of the Sistine Chapel—a confirmed atheist masquerading as the Almighty in the heartland.

Umland was a thickset, freckled-faced farm boy with red hair when he first saw Eiseley while walking across the University of Nebraska campus with Bill Gaffney, who pointed the poet out. It was a cold autumn morning, and Eiseley was standing alone in front of the Temple Theater, bareheaded, wearing a leather jacket, apparently lost in thought. Umland never forgot the impressive brow, "soaring up with a glacial whiteness."

His interest in Eiseley was more than casual. Umland was one of a circle of artists and would-be writers who hung out at the all-night restaurant in the old bus depot. These informal gatherings were usually arranged by the yet unpublished Mari Sandoz, who lived in an eight-dollar-a-month room and subsisted on stale cinnamon rolls. For the price of a cup of coffee one could talk endlessly about the *Dial*, about James Joyce, John Dos Passos, D.H. Lawrence, Sherwood Anderson and *Winesburg, Ohio*, or about *Spoon River Anthology*, *Babbit* and *Main Street*, and the outrage of H.L. Mencken on being arrested for selling a copy of the *American Mercury* in Boston. There were long discussions involving the work of local writers: poems by Loren Eiseley, his fiancée Mabel Langdon, and Weldon Kees, short stories by Pan Sterling, Dorothy Thomas, and Lowry Wimberly.

In 1928, after dropping out of the university, Umland entered a new social dimension. It seemed that half of America was on the move. Like leaves in windrows, the dispossessed gathered beside the Union Pacific, the Rock Island, the Santa Fe, the Katy. By day they sunned themselves on flatcars; by night they cooked their meager fare in blackened tin cans, then slept, with one eye open, wrapped up in old newspapers, their fires blinking like the bivouacs of great armies on the outskirts of cities under siege. Many begged their way across the country, while others stole anything that was not nailed down. They fought with bare knuckles, straight razors, and switchblade knives, had intercourse under dirty blankets in the dark corners of crowded freight cars, converged into pairs and small groups, then dispersed again, only to repeat the ritual down the line.

Umland spent the next three years bumming across forty states, Canada, and Mexico. He eventually returned to his home town of Eagle, Nebraska, where his parents had purchased a little house after retiring from the family farm. Husking nubbins and working as a hired hand soon made him restless for the open road, in spite of its hardships, so he decided to turn hobo once more.

Before departing, he stopped by Andrews Hall to tell Wimberly goodbye and give him a manuscript for the *Schooner*. The Doc, whose perplexed stare Umland never forgot, exclaimed, "You can't leave Lincoln just now. It's too damned cold to ride a boxcar!" He then told Umland about the Works Progress Administration and the need for a state editor to manage the newly established Nebraska Writer's project, which was headquartered in the Union Terminal Warehouse only a few blocks away. Though Umland had never done any editorial work, he was hired on the spot and soon found himself in charge of publishing *Nebraska: A Guide to the Cornhusker State*.

Eiseley, who was equally strapped, also signed on with Franklin Roosevelt's New Deal. As his editor, Umland assigned him the task of writing introductory essays on the geology, paleontology, and prehistoric Indian culture of the state.

As the two became better acquainted, they discovered certain parallels in their lives that a superstitious Wimberly thought belied coincidence. Both Umland and Eiseley were born in 1907 and retained memories of Halley's Comet and a bloody prison break during a great blizzard in 1912, when they were five years old; both graduated from high school in June of 1925, enrolled as freshmen at the university the following September, penned articles for the *Schooner*, and then dropped out of classes in the spring of 1928 to ride the rails for a time. Yet as Umland came to know Eiseley better, he realized that they were separated by a vast gulf of experience—and maturity.

In contrast to his campus reputation as a stoical, self-sufficient drifter, Eiseley projected a youthful shyness combined with the overly polite manners of a poet. "Most boys in Lincoln," Umland confided, "got their first work experience mowing lawns, delivering newspapers, washing windows, scrubbing floors, hoeing weeds, spading gardens, but Loren did none of these. His was a case of prolonged adolescence and as he approached maturity he seemed actually fearful of making his own way in the world." He had almost no confidence in his ability to earn a living, partly because, at age twenty-eight, he had never held a steady job. Eiseley questioned Umland again and again about his future plans. "When I told him that I had no intention of ever resuming any studies at the university to obtain a degree he couldn't believe it. He was incredulous. The WPA would end one day! What would I do then?" Indeed, there were many times when Umland literally wanted to shake Eiseley to snap out of it. Unless he obtained his Ph.D., Umland remembered thinking to himself, there was little hope that Eiseley would ever lead a halfway successful life.

Eiseley's ingrained paranoia was also much in evidence. To him, Umland later wrote me, "the world was full of two kinds of living things—the hunters and the hunted. Eiseley believed he was one of the hunted, a Steppenwolf figure." He tacked a copy of "Alone," a poem by Edgar Allan Poe, above his desk:

> *From childhood's hour I have not been*
> *As others were—I have not seen*
> *As others saw—I could not bring*
> *My passions from a common spring—*

When a fellow worker read the verse and cracked a disparaging joke, Eiseley was deeply offended.

Although intentionally vague as to both his whereabouts and the chronology of his wanderings, Eiseley claimed to have traveled the American West in boxcars, trying desperately to create the impression that between the sprawling land and endless sky he did not exist; that if he never arrived anywhere it would not have mattered. So far as Umland was concerned, the Odysseyan status Eiseley projected in his eloquent autobiographical prose forever exceeded his grasp. He doubted that Eiseley could ever have been a successful hobo; he had too much pride to beg for dinners and was simply too helpless to make it as a transient laborer. "Loren was all intellect, all abstraction. He could not have survived a long period of drifting." Nor was Eiseley inclined to speak of his wanderings with Umland, who had himself spent years being shaken up and down in boxcars, and whose book-length manuscript of life on the rails he had read with undisguised admiration. "He seemed so hesitant and vague and uncertain that we were soon talking about other matters."

Bill Gaffney, too, thought that the majority of Eiseley's journeys were taken on paper, more the product of imagination than of firsthand experience. Gaffney compared his friend with their mutual acquaintance, a roistering, carefree youth named Preston Holder, whom Eiseley very much admired: "Eiseley was rather shy and physically frail; he traveled inside cars. Holder was physically rugged and often rode the rods, or hung precariously between cars, or, in the countryside with no tunnels, rode the running boards that topped the boxcars." Lacking the courage to give the rails a try himself, Gaffney would have gladly traded places with either one.

Then came the day when Eiseley informed Wimberly that he was going to marry Mabel Langdon, a willowy fashion plate whose discriminating eye and administrative skills had won her the post of assistant curator of the university art gallery. Pulling no punches, the Doc stunned his protégé by telling him that he considered it a mistake. Mabel was not one of the outcast people that Eiseley felt a special kinship with but rather someone who could resolve his immediate problems—a safe, secure anchorage. It would not only be unfair, but extremely selfish of him to spend a lifetime drawing on

her strength while offering so little emotional sustenance in return. According to Umland, Eiseley forsook
the easy chair in Wimberly's office and the two drifted
apart after that.

It was only near the end of their guidebook work, in
the spring of 1936, that Umland gained some perspective on the psychic scars borne by his friend. The two
had gotten into the habit of taking long, mostly silent,
walks around the city during the weekends. They
wound up in Wyuka Cemetery one afternoon, where
Umland remembered standing over the grave of William Buchanan Price, Eiseley's uncle, while the latter
revealed how deeply indebted he was to the man. It was
"Buck" who had taken him on his first visit to the old
red-brick museum on the university campus; Buck who
had kept a roof over his head and that of his widowed
mother. Umland also remembered the time Eiseley
pointed to a map of Nebraska and the site in Dodge
County where his grandfather Eiseley homesteaded before the Civil War. In a rare moment of candor, Eiseley
went on to tell the story of his failed father and the
almost unbearable pain of Clyde Eiseley's tragic marriage to the deaf and neurotic Daisy Corey. Umland
finally concluded that Loren, like his mother, was a
born sufferer, and this had kept him from feeling the
slightest bit of sympathy for her. Both had been rivals
for Clyde's affection, and when he died of stomach
cancer there was no other resource to draw on.

Kenneth Forward, a diminutive, soft-spoken professor of English, told Umland of a walk he had taken with
Eiseley when Loren was a student in his class. He had
turned in a paper describing the houses in which he
had lived while growing up on Lincoln's south side. All
three homes were within a few blocks of one another;
each held painfully vivid memories of his mother's
presence. Eiseley's essay so touched Forward that he

talked his student into taking him on a tour of the neighborhood. Some years later, Forward retraced their route for Umland's benefit. When they paused in front of the Price home the curtains parted, as if on cue, and a gray face peered out. The embarrassed pair quickly turned away: "The stone-deaf woman and her sister were still living in that house," Umland recalled with a shudder. I shuddered along with Old RU in the pathos of a nearly forgotten moment. I also shared the pain of this last witness who had miraculously snatched the past from oblivion, even as he had twice sparred with Death and won a reprieve.

Thirty years passed before Umland saw Eiseley again. The now famous writer-naturalist delivered a lecture at the University of Missouri in Kansas City, where Umland happened to be living. Umland noted that Eiseley spoke with a dry seriousness developed from long years of practice. "His words cut the air with experienced incisiveness and at times soared for emphasis." They met afterward in the book-lined study of a professor. "How were Kenneth and Dorothy Forward, Preston Holder, and Bill Gaffney?" Eiseley wanted to know. He had seen the *Prairie Schooner* infrequently of late and found himself scanning the list of contributors for familiar names in vain. He was certain something symbolic could be written about the Doc and his little coterie of gifted writers, but the period was too pain-ridden for him to attempt it. Wimberly's liking for cats, ghosts, gnomes, and closet shadows meant more to him than ever. He wished he could become a fugitive from civilization, but one had to pay the rent. There must be something more than lectures, hectic flights across the country, sleepless nights in strange hotels.

While Eiseley had a marked tendency to forget old debts as well as old friends, Umland was not one to hold a man to strict accounts, especially a creative artist. He

believed that Lowry Wimberly had nurtured three gen-
iuses during the first decade of the *Schooner's* publication (1927–37): the mercurial novelist and historian,
Mari Sandoz, the dispirited, ultimately suicidal poet,
Weldon Kees, and Loren Eiseley. Yet nowhere in his
autobiography did Eiseley so much as mention either
Wimberly, who died in 1959, or the little magazine in
which he had gotten his start as a poet and essayist,
much less the time spent with Umland at the WPA. In a
hand-written letter to Martin S. Peterson, an associate
from the old days, Eiseley lamely observed, "As you
doubtless have noted, I passed over the University of
Nebraska pretty fast and it troubled me not to find a
way of getting Wimberly in without delaying the forward flow of the narrative."[2]

The Gaff had had even less contact with Eiseley over
the years, and it clearly hurt the man who, as a youth,
was too sensitive to take to the rails. He hadn't expected
to engage Eiseley in a long correspondence, but neither
was he prepared when the companion of his early
manhood wrote nothing of their mutual love of poetry
or long rambles across rolling fields laced by wind and
sun, snow and ice. When I broached this delicate subject, the limpid eyes suddenly clouded over, the ancient
pipe quivered ever so slightly and, for the first and only
time, the words failed to come. It was then that I
remembered something Eiseley was told by a black girl
while vacationing in Bimini, on the Old Spanish Main:
"Those as hunts treasure must go alone, at night, and
when they find it they have to leave a little of their blood
behind them."[3]

While Old RU and The Gaff stand out most vividly
in my mind's eye, another hundred or so hours of taped
reminiscences line the drawer of a file cabinet in my
study closet. Above them, in more manilla folders than
I care to count, are hundreds of letters and a score of

memoirs—some running to as many as twenty pages—
written for me by those who knew Loren Eiseley before
fame came calling. Without giving the matter much
thought at first, I eventually realized that I had assumed
the role of archivist as well as that of biographer, and
with it an additional set of responsibilities.

Surprisingly, very few had spurned my advances,
though some had to be gently wooed for months, even
years, before finally agreeing to speak. Sometimes they
told me things I already knew or whose veracity I
privately called into question, but mostly they breathed
life into my subject. A member of Eiseley's high school
senior class with whom he fell in love after temporarily
breaking up with Mabel supplied me with the originals
of his letters. The cancelled two-cent stamps are still
attached to the envelopes which bear the telling dates of
September and October, 1931. Another gracious lady,
who had also graduated from high school with Eiseley,
kept a stack of memorabilia which is now in one of those
manilla folders. Eiseley, the "melancholy loner," had
conveniently forgotten to mention that he was both
captain of his high school football team and president
of the senior class. He had also played the comic part of
Mr. Gear of the Speed Motor Car Company in the class
play, *Kicked out of College*. And there is little doubt that
he had a major role in selecting the class motto—"It's
better to be a live scrub than a dead thoroughbred."

So often, it is the little things one picks up in an
interview that later assume the greatest importance.
Before speaking with his classmates, I had pictured
Eiseley as an intensely serious, isolated youth whose
only friends were books—an egghead to put it bluntly.
While indeed he had his deeply serious side, a class
president nicknamed "Bozo" conjures up a rather different image. Eiseley had titled his autobiography *All
the Strange Hours*, but after completing several interviews

it occurred to me that I had better pay equally close attention to the hours that were not so strange.

I revisited Lincoln several months later, before heading south to the University of Kansas at Lawrence, where Eiseley taught from 1937 to 1944. The Gaff had kept in contact during the interim, writing me long single-spaced letters on yellow typing paper or on the back of sheets bearing the logo of the Nebraska Folklore Society. The contents were mainly concerned with additional questions I had raised following our interview. Each began with an apology for the time it took him to respond, often with a literary flourish. "I'm sorry to be so slow about things, but, as that aging navigator Ulysses remarked, 'We are not now of that strength which in old days moved earth and heaven; things slow down, down.'" It was apparent, however, that Gaffney relished the diversion and we agreed to meet when next I came to town.

It seemed that the aging ranch house had shed considerably more of its brown paint while the garden, to which I was again led by even more mincing footsteps, had grown into a deeper tangle. This time I left the recorder in the car, a circumstance noted by my host more out of curiosity than protest. I explained that he had told me everything I needed to know and that I meant this to be a social call, and so it was. When I finally got up to leave, Gaffney insisted on following me to the car. It was then that I realized he had something more on his mind. Leaning inside the window, he whispered, "Won't you come back after you finish up in Kansas?"

I realized that The Gaff's plaint had less to do with our newly established friendship than with the deep chasm of memory opened up by my queries. The biographer was about to move on, leaving an old and gentle epic poet behind to ponder his distant past. I was so moved that I dared not look him in the eye. Lawrence, I explained, while pretending to study the dried remains of a bug on the windshield, was on the interstate home. I had been away so much the past year that I couldn't spare the time. He nodded in resignation, and I watched the sea captain waver and finally disappear from the rearview mirror.

We talked by telephone once or twice after that and exchanged a few more letters, the last of which reached me in April, 1985. Shortly thereafter The Gaff's health failed and he was confined to a nursing home, too ill to receive visitors. Old RU, with whom I still correspond regularly, wrote me a brief note on Valentine's Day, 1986. "You asked me to keep you informed of Bill Gaffney's health. Bill gave up the struggle yesterday and went to join the immortals." Eiseley's line drifted back into consciousness: "Those as hunts treasure must go alone . . . and . . . have to leave a little of their blood behind them."

7

A Shiver in the Archives

In a penetrating essay titled "The Historian and His Society," J.H. Hexter lays it on the line: "A great deal of historical research and writing is stiflingly dull and unrewarding work. The vision of the historian as a sort of intellectual private eye, swashbuckling through a succession of unremittingly fascinating adventures of the mind, can survive only among those who do not destroy it by engaging in historical research."[1]

Skeptics who require support for this assertion beyond Hexter's endowed chair at an Ivy League university are invited by him to take a stroll down the corridors of any great research library where historians are wont to congregate, especially during the summer months when, in the minds of the tax-paying public, academics are "on vacation." Consider the number of scholarly drudges bent over the varnished oak tables, their disheveled heads lolling on folded arms. "They are not at the moment burning with a hard gemlike flame; they are not thinking deep and exciting thoughts; they are sleeping off their ennui."[2] Like true detectives, who little resemble Sherlock Holmes, these denizens of the archives have driven themselves into sweet oblivion by pursuing false leads down cold trails to dead ends, by amassing bulging but frequently useless dossiers, and by probing dull monographs whose authors bought more discount copies as Christmas gifts for their in-laws than were purchased by all the libraries in the land.

Yet sometimes there comes a great notion—or at least access to one. I remember vividly a week spent in the archives of the American Philosophical Society, founded by Benjamin Franklin's Junto and located no more than a stone's throw from Philadelphia's Independence Hall. Long days of grubbing through boxes crammed with old letters had yielded only a single document worth quoting, and that of dubious merit. Without my knowing it, the pain and discouragement were beginning to show. Just before my final departure, the sensitive young archivist in charge asked if I would like to see a few of the more historically valuable objects secreted in the vault. I could hardly refuse, although none of them had any bearing on my scholarly pursuit.

She returned, a few minutes later, with three items that resurrected the lost schoolboy in the man. Before me lay one of the original copies of Jefferson's Declaration of Independence, drafted only blocks from the place where I now sat and ratified but footsteps away. I next opened what appeared to be a small leather folder and discovered a finely tooled pocket chessboard, once the property of the great Franklin himself. Ben and his compatriots had played the game with miniature tokens fashioned from the ivory of a harpooned whale. Finally, there were the beautifully crafted journals of Meriwether Lewis and William Clark, who nearly starved to death while fulfilling Jefferson's wish that they chart a land route to the Pacific. The blood-red ink used to highlight details on the maps served as a melancholy reminder that Lewis, who was appointed governor of the Louisiana Territory in 1807, had died under mysterious circumstances in a lonely inn on the Natchez Trace. Even so, my elation was such that I stepped into the light of a late summer's afternoon and took a salutatory turn around Independence Hall, then kept right on going—briefcase, books, and all—until I reached distant Rittenhouse Square, the biographical fires rekindled by these wonderful objects from afar.

The last time I had felt such exultation as a scholar was years earlier in a distant archive. After many months of planning and background research, I was about to pay my first visit to the Rare Manuscripts Room of Cambridge University Library. I slept fitfully the night before and awakened, wide-eyed, at dawn in the small second-floor bedroom I had rented for £30 a month in a gray row house on French's Road, a *cul-de-sac* some two miles from my objective. It was the middle of January, and the only source of warmth was a small space heater that devoured coins at a voracious clip, then promptly went on strike in the small hours for lack of sustenance. My first sight on this morning was that of my own breath, and in the coming weeks I would often linger motionless beneath the covers, mesmerized by the zigzagging rivulets of condensation on the windowpane. Fortunately, adrenalin is a potent antifreeze. With a contempt for the elements worthy of my Viking forbears, I leaned into a biting wind and arrived at the CUL just a minute or two after opening.

The hormonal flow was abruptly stanched by the visage of a wizened clerk who met me at the door. He displayed not the vaguest interest in my mission, nor in the letters of introduction I pressed into his arthritic hand. I was told to wait on a bench in the cloakroom until someone could see me. "Have you a shilling?" he queried. I fumbled in my pocket and produced the silver coin, since outmoded by Britain's switch to the decimal system. He pointed in the direction of some lockers and told me to put everything I was carrying

inside, then disappeared down a hallway with my un-
opened envelopes.

Protocol! In my exuberance I had forgotten about
the formalities. Yet I had written ahead, as is required
by archives throughout Europe, and felt certain that the
doors would soon open for me. After all, the English
are well known in the intellectual community for their
cooperative attitude; it is the French one has to be
concerned about. (One authority advises the researcher
going to Paris to be prepared for a week's struggle with
the bureaucracy. In addition to a passport, supply yourself with a birth certificate, a university diploma, your
mother's marriage license, and a letter from your ambassador. A return ticket home is guaranteed to have a
soothing effect.[3]) Nevertheless, sitting there on display
like the class dunce reminded me of Bret Harte's obser-
vation on the defective moral quality of being a stranger.

Several minutes passed before I was collected by the
doorkeeper and shown into the paneled office of an
equally ancient gnome whose thinning silver locks
grazed his hunched shoulders. He pointed to a chair in
front of his massive desk and then, to my discomfort,
began reading out loud from the file containing my
permissions request. When he finished, his gray eyes
began to twinkle and his thin lips curved upward in a
wry smile. "Well, well, young sir, an ambitious quest
yours—most ambitious indeed." Although I was in my
mid-thirties and a full professor, I looked much
younger, indeed was often mistaken for a student. Forcing a wan smile of my own, I nodded in agreement
while recalling a similar reaction on the part of the
customs official who had queried me about the purpose
of my visit to his country. When I attempted to explain
he betrayed himself with a look of incredulity yet waived
me through without comment, obviously thinking that

no one bent on serious mischief would concoct such a zany ruse.

The gnome reached for a pen and filled out a small blue card—my coveted passport to the archives—which he then handed over to me. I noticed that it was scheduled to expire within six weeks, about half the time I planned to be in Cambridge. When I protested, he explained that this was standard procedure. If, at the end of the period, I wished to apply for an extension there should be no problem, provided, of course, I was still around. With that cheerful benediction I was escorted to the hall and shown the elevator that would bear me to the threshold of the sanctum sanctorum.

My frayed nerves sustained another jolt the moment I stepped into the great room. "If you can't do it right," an Olympian voice boomed from somewhere overhead, "then there is no use doing it a'tall; not a'tall! Do you understand?" For a moment I thought the blast had been directed at me, the more so because it was followed by absolute silence. However, a glance at the passive faces of those seated at the great oak tables told me that this was not an unusual occurrence. Indeed, I would soon learn that the voice belonged to the dyspeptic senior editor of the Darwin correspondence, who, along with a small staff of overworked assistant editors and harried scriveners, was just beginning the monumental task of compiling a projected two score or more volumes of every letter written by the master of Down House, a labor that seems destined to continue well into the next century. Strangely, that great anvil of a voice has remained forever disembodied in my mind, for not once in all the time I spent at the CUL was I destined to lay eyes on its source, which is doubtless just as well.

The sublibrarian, whose diminutive stature and puckish features reminded me of the comedic actor Dudley Moore, had been alerted to my arrival by telephone. He introduced himself as Allan Purvis and proceeded to brief me on the rules governing the use of the collection, which are fairly standard throughout the archival world. I would be allowed no more than one box of material at a time, which must be called up at least half an hour in advance on special slips of paper available at the desk. Pen and ink were strictly forbidden; I could bring my own pencils, but it would be just as well if I used theirs. Also banned from the reading room were briefcases, file folders, and tablets of every kind. I must provide my own sheets of blank paper which the staff had the right to examine without notice. Nor were coats, umbrellas, or other forms of apparel allowed. Finally, talking was *verboten*.

I consulted the loose-leaf catalogue and filled out the first of what eventually became dozens of acquisition slips, then took a seat at an unoccupied table. Having promised, in the interests of Anglo-American relations, to keep me waiting no longer than necessary, Purvis disappeared into the mazelike stacks behind the desk, leaving a more junior colleague in charge. He returned, minutes later, with a large box and signaled me to come forward. I suddenly felt the same rush of adrenalin as before, partly because I knew what the carton held but also because of its color—a sanguine tone that stirred a biographer's memory.

Even though Isaac Newton died a wealthy man, little beyond his land and financial holdings had any intrinsic worth. Indeed, the most striking thing about his earthly goods is that the normally staid Newton immersed himself in a veritable sea of crimson. He slept on a crimson mohair bed hung with matching "Harrateen" curtains; the tall windows of his house in Kensington were adorned with crimson drapes topped by crimson valances; crimson mohair hangings covered the walls. In the dining room was a crimson "satee," and in the back parlor a crimson easy chair with six crimson cushions comforted the aging master of the Mint on his return from the Tower.[4] In his youth, Newton had concocted multiple recipes for red ink by employing such ingredients "ye clearest blood of a sheepe."[5] Years later, as Cambridge's newly appointed Lucasian Professor, the twenty-seven-year-old Newton donned the scarlet and ermine robes that distinguished him from the lesser teaching fellows and delivered his first lecture during the Lenten Term. Although the color of the boxes may have been nothing more than coincidence, I preferred to think that some librarian with the soul of an artist had done his research well.

I followed my usual practice of working through the lunch hour, but little of a scholarly nature would be accomplished this day or, for that matter, during the next several days to come. Too many emotions needed to be brought under control, too much daydreaming needed to be done. Two dozen reels of microfilm containing Newton's other scattered writings had not even remotely prepared me for this humbling and ultimately inexpressible moment. The French scientist Joseph Louis Lagrange once remarked that Newton was the luckiest man to have ever lived. There is but one universe and one set of laws to be discovered. It was Newton's supreme fortune to have been that person. In my unsteady hands were now the very fiber and ink present at the creation—the diagrams of prismatic experiments that had enabled Newton to separate white light into its constituent parts, the hypotheses and mathematical proofs that had permitted genius to track the rhythmic course of planets and stars, number holding sway above the flux. Here the sacred precepts of a new and wondrous age, as inviolate in their own right as the prophecies of old.

As the days passed and the call slips began to pile

up, I grew increasingly uneasy, especially when I reviewed my meager notes before going to bed each night. If I hoped to get anything done, it was obvious that I must find a means of putting the documents and the man who created them into a less rarefied perspective. As I kept telling myself, equations and diagrams alone do not a biography make. Bizarre as it may seem, I began to focus not on the product of genius, which was overwhelming in the abstract, but on the more human traits associated with the papers.

To begin with, there was the handwriting itself. In a commonplace book from his undergraduate years at Trinity College, Newton employed an elegant classical script befitting the notes he took in Greek from Aristotle's *Organon* and *Nicomachean Ethics*. Then, at some point in 1663, he skipped several dozen pages before beginning another, radically different, set of entries. He titled this section *Quaestiones quaedam Philosophicae* (*Certain Philosophical Questions*) and at the top of the first page penned a line that summarized to perfection his conversion to the new order: "Amicus Plato amicus Aristoteles magis amica veritas." ("I am a friend of Plato, I am a friend of Aristotle, but truth is my greater friend.")[6] Concurrently, the script of Newton's youth yielded to a simpler, more utilitarian hand, which, with occasional modifications, was to remain Newton's for the rest of his life.

Then, too, there was the sheer magnitude of the intellectual labors. In addition to the published works Newton left thousands of pages and many millions of words in manuscript. In the heightened consciousness of genius the mind insisted on expressing itself; it would not be silenced. It would speak even if spoke on paper to itself alone. Except for some highly personal letters, Newton preserved every variety of written material imaginable: random jottings, adolescent notebooks, and book-length manuscripts were all treated like Holy Writ. (A critical early equation on gravity was overlooked by scholars for centuries because it was written on the back of a lease entered into by his mother.) The interminable recopying of long documents—five, ten, fifteen, or even twenty times over—may be taken as evidence of self-conscious awe and of a struggle for perfection. Isaac Newton knew well the words of the ancient prophet Isaiah: "Precept upon precept, precept upon precept; line upon line, line upon line; here a little and there a little." (28:10).

The quantity of material in the red boxes also spoke eloquently to another of Newton's traits. Like a prophet in the wilderness, the natural philosopher severed most of his ties to the outside world and substituted the great outflow of his mind for the human contacts required by those who possess no such profound resource. A virtual recluse while living in Cambridge, he was at home only within the narrow but sanctified confines of his silent study next to Trinity's Great Gate, where the ideas doubled and tripled like so much mental yeast. When, as an aged icon, Newton was asked how he made his discoveries, a Puritan's candor could easily have been mistaken for a jest: "By always thinking unto them."

Newton's London stationer, whoever he may have been, was surely delighted, if somewhat puzzled, by the Lucasian Professor's large and frequent purchase orders. Although Newton was very careful with his money, he kept an eye on posterity and bought only the finest writing paper. Two and one-half centuries of England's chill and damp have exacted no greater toll than a bit of pleasant foxing at the margins; the ink seems to have faded hardly at all. For diversion I traced the water-mark, which consists of a lion rampant and the slogan *Pro Patria*—for the fatherland—to Jean Villedary, a French Huguenot who fled to Holland after Louis XIV revoked the Edict of Nantes.[7] What a royal mistake to have made fugitives of men like Jean Villedary!

What a contrast between the craftsman's beautiful rag pages and those torn from a cheap legal tablet on which I was taking notes. Exposure to light and air was certain to render my scrawl illegible within two or three years, not that it would matter to anyone but myself. On the other hand, if my finished manuscript did not get printed on acid free paper, little of it beyond a brittle memory would survive the coming century. Such depressing thoughts resulted in a moral lapse. I sometimes broke the house rules by lightly running my fingertips over Newton's script, hoping to be transported back to the den of the lion by osmosis, where nothing disturbed the reverie save the scratch, scratch, scratch of a feather pen.

The weather grew worse as winter in the fens wore on. Temperatures hovered just above freezing, which kept the incessant rain from turning into what would have been to me, a footbound midwesterner, welcome snow. I made my way back and forth to an even colder room, a round trip of four miles, and watched in curious detachment while my weight dropped. Dining, normally one of my greatest pleasures, had become an ordeal, mainly because it meant going out again at night to one of the few restaurants that remained open after six. Most of these establishments were Indian or Pakistani; the heavily spiced dishes caused my stomach to rebel. I settled into the habit of carrying a sack of bakery goods home in the evenings or walking the two blocks to the residence of a gregarious young Filipino who sold undercooked fried chicken and chips to go. The wrappings were always saturated with grease by the time I was ready to eat, and I shudder now to think what my cholesterol level must have been had my doctor con-

cerned himself with such matters at that time. Worse
still was the unshakable head cold that dogged my
existence for nearly two months. Hot, soaking baths
would have done wonders for my condition, but the tap
water was lukewarm on the best of days and turned icy
before covering the bottom of the tub. Perhaps out of
spite, I purchased a copy of Defoe's fictional *Journal of
the Plague Year* at Blackwell's and took perverse pleasure
at the suffering of London's besieged citizenry. I also
thought of all those starving, garret-bound French novelists and painters of the nineteenth century who either
succumbed to tuberculosis or committed suicide. It was
no longer clear to me that nobility and suffering for
one's art are synonymous. One evening, on my way back
to my room in the dark, I was foolishly caught in a
downpour without an umbrella, and remember ducking
into the Gothic entry of one of the colleges on Trinity
Street to await its passing. From a room overlooking the
inner court came the muted skirling of a bagpipe, so
poignant and so melancholy that a tear formed for
memories of home.

I had made the mistake of failing to establish some
sort of affiliation with one of the colleges, which, now
that I look back on it, would not have been very difficult.
But I was a bit naive; besides, Cambridge intimidated
me; gaining access to such hallowed ground had seemed
sufficient unto itself. I also avoided contact with certain
members of the intellegentsia, most especially a gifted
historian of mathematics. This editor of Newton's mathematical papers, which run to a daunting eight volumes,
had left initialed notes scattered throughout the red
boxes. Simultaneously lecturing a dead Newton, the
library staff, and future scholars on a multitude of
computational and clerical errors, D.T.W. was clearly a
force to be reckoned with.

Luckily, I was befriended by Allan Purvis, who invited me to his home for dinner one Sunday afternoon. We drove out to see Ely cathedral later in the day, accompanied by the archivist's wife and little boy. The great gray stones radiated cold like chunks of glacial ice, a harsh reminder that for a time the greatest threat to the monks of northern Christendom was neither the Devil nor the Vikings, but winter's fatal thrall. When the child began to shiver and cry he spoke for all of us, and we happily retreated to the warmth of the family hearth.

As any scholar worth his salt can attest, archives are a resource whose utility is heavily dependent on the knowledge and complaisance of their custodians. Like the rest of us, archivists come in every size, shape, and temperament. And as in every profession, there are some bad apples among the good. My particular choice for Scrooge of the Year is the archivist who has become so attached to a collection that he thinks of it as his own, much like the librarian who tips his hand by grimacing when you check out more than three books at a time. On balance, however, archivists are a species who take the greatest pleasure from helping you find what you want. Demonstrate your sincerity by good cheer and deference and you will be pointed in directions you never dreamed existed, while nettling restrictions will suddenly disappear, rules will bend, and deadlines will be overlooked. Alienate the gatekeeper by assuming an insolent air and you may rightly find yourself banished to an intellectual Siberia.

I marked an anniversary by knocking on the office door of the little man who had issued my blue library card, now about to expire. Trying not to appear smug, I asked that my privileges be extended for another six weeks. To my surprise, he reached into my file and pulled out a completed pass, which he handed over with a wink. I was not the only one doing my homework.

By this time I had made considerable headway on the manuscripts, especially after Alan informed me that the irreplaceable documents were eligible for photocopying, something I had never thought possible. Happy as I was to acquire a portable archives at the equivalent of about ten cents a page, I couldn't help but ponder the consequences of exposing such ancient paper and ink to the camera's blinding eye.

No sooner had I resolved this problem than another faced me. Although I was working in the heart of a great library containing almost every volume written by Newton and his contemporaries, the collection was all but useless to me. Unlike the standard card catalogue which, until recently, was a fixture in every American library, the CUL, like the Bodleian at Oxford and London's British Museum, has its own peculiar filing system, with roots stretching back into the Middle Ages. To penetrate its mysteries, I would have needed full-time assistance from the staff.

Those who have done battle with the new computer cataloguing will know exactly what I mean. Many of our libraries are now on radically different systems, too many of which were purchased when this technology was in its infancy. Days of practicing on the computer terminal may be required before competency is achieved, virtually denying access to the visiting scholar on a deadline.

As it happened, I was spending more and more time at Trinity College's Wren Library, where a substantial portion of Newton's books and bound pamphlets are located in an alcove overlooked by Bertel Thorwaldsen's statue of Byron, an offering once declined by the Dean of Westminster Abbey on the grounds that the poet had led a disolute life. Newton's volumes are heavily annotated, providing small but important clues to his intellectual development. He was also in the habit of dog-earing pages, though not in the conventional manner. Rather than simply fold down the corner, he bent the page so that it pointed directly to the passage he wished to recall. Even after a corner has been returned to its normal position the telltale crease remains.

To reach the Wren is to pass through the still living archives of Newton's day. Trinity, bordered on one side by St. John's and on the other by Caius, was, in the words of the seventeenth-century scholar Thomas Fuller, "the stateliest and most uniform Colledge in Christendom."[8] On the massive exterior of the Great Gate, which faces Trinity Street, is the statue of the college's founder, Henry VIII. From the interior steps of the towering entrance the visitor gains a commanding view of the Great Court built in the reign of Elizabeth I at the instigation of Thomas Nevile, Trinity's ambitious master. Nevile had the court enclosed by Tudor Gothic facades which connect the Chapel, Master's Lodge, and magnificent Dining Hall, with its hammer-and-beam ceiling, minstrels' gallery, and domineering portrait of Henry, which takes six strong men to carry, the same number, I surmised, needed to move the bloated monarch about after the onset of gross obesity and gout. Newton came to Trinity in the spring of 1661 as a sizar, a lowly station that required him to perform such menial tasks as running errands, waking his fellow students for morning chapel before dawn, polishing boots, and waiting tables beneath Henry's imperious gaze. He would rise to occupy an endowed chair and reside in the most coveted rooms in the college—E 4 Great Court. The second floor apartment, located just to the north of the Great Gate, overlooks Trinity Street; the steps leading up to it are popularly known as Newton's Staircase.

Trinity's cloistered precincts did much to mend my tattered spirits. Here had trodden the poets John Dryden, Alfred Lord Tennyson, and Byron, who was occasionally seen in the company of his pet bear, which he kept in a stable in the Ram Yard. Ernest Rutherford, the first to split the atom, was a Trinity man, as were Francis Bacon, Nehru of India, philosophers Alfred North Whitehead, Ludwig Wittgenstein and Bertrand Russell, the jurist Sir Edward Coke, the novelist William Makepeace Thackeray, historians G.M. Trevelyan, Lords Acton and Macaulay, and the not-to-be forgotten children's poet A.A. Milne, author of *Winnie-the-Pooh*. Occasionally, as I passed through the undergraduate library on my way to the Wren, I paused to scan the intense young faces and wondered which of them would be numbered one day among the blessed.

In contrast to most libraries in the States, the stacks of the Wren were closed, requiring that I fill out a call slip for each work I wanted to consult. Luckily, the card catalogue proved more tractable than that of the CUL, and I quickly discovered that almost every book I required for background research, however obscure, was part of the collection. Since I was the only scholar on the premises, librarian John Gaskell graciously accorded me carte blanche. The books were fetched by a tall, angular junior assistant, who became embarrassingly apologetic if it took him more than twenty minutes to deliver a volume, many of which had the feel of the tomb. When I asked about this, the young man explained that the library's collection had overflowed the main building long ago and was parceled out in unheated structures nearby. Glancing at his thin sweater, I suddenly felt a twinge of guilt and never sent him out more than once a day after that.

The Wren itself, so beautiful that old scholars, like old elephants, should go there to die, could not have been more than fifty-five degrees, a harsh contrast to the climate-controlled Rare Manuscripts Room. Two

pairs of socks, two shirts, and a heavy cardigan did little
to stave off the chill. I sat by the hour with only my heels
touching the freezing marble floor, entertaining visions
of Bob Cratchit adding up Scrooge's fat accounts in
fingerless gloves.

One morning, a member of the staff placed a large
box of papers on the three-hundred-year-old table opposite mine. She then left, only to return minutes later
with a rectangular object, the sight of which made my
thick blood course. Kneeling down, she inserted a plug
in the socket beneath her wooden bench and situated
the space heater in such a way that her feet rested
squarely upon its metal frame. I spent the remainder of
the morning calculating the odds. Trinity was already
treating me with great deference; to show my gratitude
by asking yet another favor might be risking too much.
Pieter Rysbrack's nearby bust of a distracted Newton,
his shirt defiantly open at the neck like that of a romantic poet basking in the Mediterranean sun, did nothing
to bolster my confidence. On the other hand, I could
hardly do justice to my subject by succumbing to pneumonia.

Had you chanced to be one of the occasional visitors
to the Wren in the weeks that followed, you might
remember having gazed upon a lone historian of the
type described by Jack Hexter. He was not burning with
a hard gemlike flame nor thinking deep and exciting
thoughts; yet, truth to tell, neither was he sleeping off
ennui. Head bowed as if in silent prayer, he was luxuri-
ating in the warm breeze wafting up his pant legs while
daydreaming of the fresh salads waiting to be eaten
back home.

Six years later, it was inner rather than outer
weather that drove me, shivering, from the archives into
the brilliance of the noonday sun. It was a summer's day

in 1984, the biography of Newton having been published the previous March. Even as the reviews continued to trickle in, I was deep into the research for a
biography of Loren Eiseley, and in surroundings mark-
edly different from those I had encountered in Albion.

Notwithstanding the fact that I had addressed my
letters of inquiry to the North Arcade, Franklin Field, it
never dawned on me that any university, let alone the
University of Pennsylvania—a member of the Ivy
League—would actually house its archives beneath the
bleachers of a football stadium. The day after my arrival
in West Philadelphia found me circling the huge structure in seriocomic bewilderment, vainly searching for a
neoclassical edifice like the others sprinkled about campus. Passersby were equally puzzled when I asked for
directions. Running out of patience, I decided to circle
the stadium once more before surrendering to a phone
booth. Suddenly there it was, high up on the northwest
corner, at the point where the less privileged wind up
viewing football games through army surplus binocu-
lars: "University of Pennsylvania Archives" read the
small black and white sign. Muttering thanks to Clio, I
pushed a gray button, waited for the sound of the
electronic door release, and climbed the echoing metal
steps to the second floor.

In keeping with their title—"Lectures at Colleges
and Other Institutions"—boxes 5 and 6 of the Eiseley
papers did not make for scintillating reading. Yet I felt
duty bound to at least scan every one of their several
hundred pages, looking for what I did not know. It was
nearing the lunch hour, which I had planned to skip,
when I began to shudder, as if someone had trodden
on my grave. At first glance, the document that trig-
gered the involuntary spasms seemed innocuous
enough. Robert Isaac White, President of Kent State
University, had written to confirm the arrangements for

Eiseley's June commencement address. But it was the
following passage, dated April 29, 1970, that chilled me
to the marrow:

> I trust that none of the 'ruckuses' at the University of
> Pennsylvania which have occasionally made the newspa-
> pers have brushed you. We have had our own problems
> and tensions but, so far, no traumatic eruption. Obvi-
> ously, I dare not speak with any confidence since, these
> days, it is hardly possible to be sure from one day to the
> next what will take place.[9]

The abstract suddenly became real as time's arrow
flung me back to a point where history and my own life
had collided. During my graduate student days at Pittsburgh's Carnegie Mellon University, I had taken part in
the civil rights marches on Washington, D.C., and in the
antiwar movement whose ranks were destined to swell
because of the tragedy about to unfold. The day after
White, a quiet gentleman-scholar, wrote to Eiseley, President Nixon informed the public via a nationally tele-
vised news conference of his decision to support a major
South Vietnamese military sweep into Cambodia. American advisors were to accompany the troops, who were
also promised heavy air and artillery support from U.S.
forces. Campus reaction across the country was swift
and furious. At Kent State, rallying students tossed fire
bombs into the rickety ROTC building and chanted
slogans while it was reduced to a heap of charred
timbers. Mayor Leroy Satrom, his townspeople in an
uproar and twenty-member police force on the verge of
cracking, requested that Governor James Rhodes send
in the National Guard. The Governor was eager to
oblige, having made campus demonstrations a key issue
in his get-tough campaign for the U.S. Senate. On May
4 a salvo from guardsmen standing atop a knoll familiar
to trysters as Blanket Hill left four students dead and

another ten wounded, including a youth paralyzed from the waist down by a bullet in the spine.

If I was ever skeptical that the Fates sometimes leave footprints, this simple letter erased all doubt. So powerful was the flood of personal memory that I desperately wanted to pick up a phone and alert President White to the specter stalking his campus. Ironically, Eiseley, who was out of town lecturing when the missive arrived, did not open the letter until after the shootings. In his reply of May 7, he more than hinted that he was no longer the man for the job, if, indeed, spring commencement was still on. "I am not a firebrand and I am not sympathetic to the turn that student protests are taking," he asserted. "This does not mean that I am indifferent to young aspirations, but I feel that however it came about it is now very difficult to reason satisfactorily with a generation which in many ways seems to reject reason."[10] White, his campus closed by court order, provided Eiseley with the exit he was seeking: "I do believe we have to walk through the door you opened with regard to your appearing at this commencement."[11] As I was to learn during the coming months, this was not quite the end of the story.

"The hippies," Eiseley scrawled in one of his several notebooks, "are a symptom of societal illness."[12] Writing to an old friend, he lamented, "I find the increasing student chaos and erosion of standards distasteful. In short, I think we are going to hell in a hand basket."[13]

Never one to engage in the cut and thrust of academic politics, Eiseley overcame his natural reserve and took part in a heated Faculty Senate debate in November 1966. At issue was the question—engendered by bitterness over the Vietnam War—of whether university research funded by the Department of Defense should remain classified. Eiseley rose to speak against a motion favoring public disclosure, citing the Western Allies' lack of preparation when Germany introduced mustard gas in World War I. He concluded: "[I]n a world such as exists around us all of the choices are grey . . . and no one [can] escape the burdens of this century by washing his hands like Pilate."[14] A friend present that day recalled that Eiseley "greatly offended" many of his colleagues by invoking the image of the hated Procurator of Judea, and the vote went against him by a considerable margin.[15]

There is no question that Eiseley considered himself as besieged as the Penn campus. The institution that had stood four-square behind the Hoover administration during his graduate school days, and was still considered the most conservative of the Ivys, had suddenly gone berserk. In 1968 alone the student body had chosen to be addressed by Muhammed Ali, who was engaged in a pitched legal battle with the Selective Service; by the atheist Madalyn Murray O'Hair; by Dr. Margaret Mead, staff-carrying guru of the Left; by Harrison Salisbury, managing editor of *The New York Times*, who called for a halt to the U.S. bombing of North Vietnam; by co-defendants Dr. Benjamin Spock and the Rev. William Sloane Coffin, Jr., who were being prosecuted by the federal government for abetting draft resisters; and by presidential hopeful Eugene J. McCarthy, who promised a crowd numbering 10,000 that, if elected, he would fire the hard-bitten hero of the conservatives, J. Edgar Hoover.

While the Vietnam Week Committee was planting 80 crosses on the lawn fronting College Hall, which a nostalgic Eiseley remembered as once being mowed by a horse-drawn sickle, the editors of the 1969 *Record*, Penn's student yearbook, were plotting another coup. Protest pictures upstaged the usual fare, including that of a naked man and woman on their knees in passionate embrace. The staff of the campus newspaper, the *Daily*

Pennsylvanian, chose to be photographed through the window of a gutted building, thus demonstrating their solidarity with the largely black and poor citizens of West Philadelphia. Faced with the "hard reality" that traditional courses had failed, the paper decided to sponsor a series of experimental seminars described as "gradeless, creditless confrontations between faculty and students that serve to expand the minds and consciousness of both parties." These included McLuhan's Attempt to Crack the Nerve of the Square World, Confronting the Establishment, Political Victims in America, and, oddly enough, The Campus Chef, which was "open to both sexes."[16]

Froelich Rainey, director of the University Museum, and Eiseley had been friends too long to nurture grudges, but their relationship became strained whenever the subject of the student protesters came up. Rainey remembered Eiseley's amazement when he invited a group of demonstrators to come inside the museum and air their grievances in the auditorium. When he tried to persuade his colleague that discourse was preferable to broken windows and bloodied faces, Eiseley just shook his head and ducked out a side door.[17]

Led by Students for a Democratic Society, an estimated 400 demonstrators occupied College Hall in February 1969. Protesting everything from the chopping down of trees to the removal of black families in the wake of campus expansion, the students held their ground for six days, forcing the cancellation of classes. Mindful of the violent debacle that had taken place at Columbia the previous spring, President Gaylord Harnwell succeeded in forging a compromise which saw the protesters emerge from the administration building singing, "Amen, Amen."

There was blood in Eiseley's eye. He fumed to his wife, Mabel, that it was high time they get out of Phila-

delphia and phoned an old friend back in his native
Lincoln, Nebraska, to inquire about the local real estate
market. The prospect came to nothing when Eiseley
was informed that the disease he was seeking to escape
had recently spread to the University of Nebraska campus.[18] Eiseley, who had applied for and been granted
an occupational deferment during World War II (although not an M.D. he taught anatomy at the University
of Kansas School of Medicine), next wrote a patriotic
letter to Commander-in-Chief Richard Nixon, who,
ironically, owed his recent election to the massive antiwar demonstrations which turned Chicago's 1968 Democratic National Convention into a bloody fiasco. Decry-
ing the erosion of America's resolve, Eiseley was
counting on his president to set things to rights. "It
appears to me that from Peru to Asia we are indeed
beginning to justify the appellation 'paper tiger' with all
the consequences present and to come that this invites."
He realized that the President's job was being made
more difficult by the widespread social unrest, which fit
perfectly his conspiracy theory of history: "Many people, particularly the young, are the more or less innocent dupes of unseen elements making use of the mass
media for the purposes of propaganda." Nevertheless,
he concluded by pleading with Nixon to do everything
within his power "to retard this uncomfortable ebbing
away of our power and purpose"; it "will be appreciated
by at least one humble American who voted for you."[19]

By the time these many facts became known to me,
the pieces were beginning to fit. The campus "ruck-
uses," as Robert White so innocently termed the student
demonstrations across the land, had indeed brushed
Eiseley, and were about to do so again. Some of the
National Guardsmen involved in what society now re-
members simply as Kent State evidenced no regret. "It's
about time we showed the bastards who's in charge,"

one soldier told a reporter from *Newsweek*. Many of the citizens of Kent, Ohio, were similarly quoted.[20] And when, at last, I got around to reading an archival copy of Eiseley's obituary from the *Philadelphia Inquirer*, the old chill returned with a vengeance, racing up my spine and standing the hairs on the back of my neck on end. When word of the fatal shootings reached Eiseley, he had turned to a friend and remarked, "They got what they asked for."[21]

8

Tools of the Trade

$\mathbf{A}$re biographers, like athletes, born I sometimes wonder? I was seven years old when my Grandfather Christianson died. He had risen in the small hours to get a drink of water, or so he told Grandmother Anna as he was leaving their large brass bed. Moments later, she heard a great crash in the dining room. The doctor who signed the death certificate told my father that Antone, who everyone called "Tony," had suffered a coronary thrombosis; he was dead before he hit the floor.

Grandfather and I had hunted night crawlers together only hours before; as usual, he held the flashlight and I grabbed. A heavy April rain assured our success; we quickly filled two Butternut coffee cans and went to bed dreaming of the fish we would catch on the weekend. Grandfather's love of fishing was natural for a man who had spent his childhood on the banks of a fjord in Norway. The only thing he liked better than fishing was eating his catch, and that too we had done the night before. Grandmother Anna, an unusually tiny woman with a painfully bent spine, disliked the smell of frying perch, so my mother had prepared supper and Grandfather ate with us. Mother later fretted that the fish she had served might have somehow played a part in Grandfather's death, but it hadn't. He was dead before he hit the floor.

A strange thing happened when my parents came into my upstairs bedroom at dawn to tell me that my fishing days with Grandfather Tony were over—forever. I don't remember crying, either then or later at the funeral, my first. But as I lay there in the gray light, I suddenly realized that someday everyone who knew Grandfather would also be gone: Grandmother Anna, Father, Mother, Uncle Kenneth, Aunt Mary Ellen, Aunt Ella, the neighbors, Reverend Weikel, Grandfather's fishing buddies, the barber Roy Cannoy, who cut his thinning hair—all of them. I would be the only one left to remember, the last person on earth to have known who Grandfather Tony was. The last one to have seen him alive. Then, after a while, I too would die, and Grandfather would truly be no more.

It was a lot of responsibility for a seven-year-old. My first thought was to write down everything I could remember about Grandfather, his looks, his funny way of speaking—which I later learned was an accent—the talks we had while fishing together, his love of the movies, the green "Willy" he drove fast whenever I asked him to, while Grandmother gesticulated and shrieked from the back seat, everything. I arose and tore a page from my thick tablet with the head of an Indian chief on its cover, then printed carefully across the top: *Grandfather Tony*. There was much to write, but the words came slowly. The sun was shining brightly before I had completed more than a few sentences, an unacknowledged harbinger of many such mornings to come. I simply lacked the words to describe the many visions in my head. The writing would have to wait; for now, memory alone must suffice. Someday, after I was grown, I would sail the ocean in reverse and seek out the family Grandfather had left behind, perhaps even try my luck in the fjord next to the village of my ancestors.

And so I remembered. Grandfather was a thickset Scandinavian, with precious little hair and pale blue eyes, not at all like the great, blond, bearded Norsemen portrayed in the movies. He was quick to laugh, loved to tell jokes and, when I stayed overnight, challenged me to drinking contests over breakfast. He was the only adult I knew who loved milk and, by being the first one to drain his glass, he taught me that children do not always win. At night, he often sat in a wicker rocking chair with his spectacles on, a huge leatherbound volume resting on his lap. I sometimes peered over his shoulder, but the print was fine, the words longer than any I had ever seen. Father told me that he was reading a law book and had always dreamt of becoming an attorney. There were family rumors that he had been swindled by a brother and his clever lawyer in a business deal, and I later surmised that Grandfather was preparing himself should he ever get the chance to go to court again.

We fished in a pit north of town, full of bullheads and sunfish. It was made clear to me in polite but firm language which pole and tackle were mine and which were Grandfather's. He threw the sunfish back—"Not worth cleaning," he groused—and laughed every time he reeled in a fat bullhead. Rather than put them on a stringer, he simply tossed them further up the bank to be collected in a gunny sack when it was time to go. I watched the heaving yellow bellies out of the corner of my eye and worried at their suffering, but Grandfather didn't mind a bit. I consoled myself by thinking that it must have been something he had learned while still a boy himself.

He often went fishing with his friends on Spirit Lake, made famous in a novel of the same name by MacKinlay Kantor. There was Sven Hesla, Edgar Eastman, Carl Grohdall and others whose names I no longer remember, European immigrants all, men whose long and tortuous paths had converged in an Iowa village so small that its streets were unnamed. One afternoon they pulled up in front of my grandparents' house in two cars, the trunks full of iced fish beyond the counting. Word quickly spread and it seemed that half the town gathered on the lawn. The old men were beaming; their days weren't over yet; they could still provide. How proud I was, unlike Grandmother, who wilted at the thought of having to fry all those smelly fish during the months to come.

Once the circus came to our village, one ring and one ancient elephant that took popcorn from my hand with the delicacy of a socialite. My grandparents and I watched the show while sitting on a blanket, and applauded loudly when a lady in red tights lay down beneath the beast and disappeared under its pendulous belly.

The whole family went to church together on Christmas Eve, after which each child received a present and a bag of candy containing a perfectly shaped apple all the way from the state of Washington. One year Grandfather gave me a jackknife and silver chain, which Mother promptly put away for safety's sake until I was "older." (As I remember, "older" never came.) We opened our other presents that same night, because that is how it had always been done in the "old country." The Christmas after Grandfather died was a terrible disappointment to me. Instead of buying the usual fresh-cut pine, Grandmother set up a small artificial tree she had ordered from the "wish book," otherwise known as the Sears-Roebuck catalog. Worse still, the tree was painted white and covered with spung glass called angel hair, which cut your finger when you tried to touch the ornaments. My parents must have felt the same as I, for after that we opened most of our presents at home on Christmas morning under a real pine.

Like Father and Uncle Kenneth, Grandfather wore maroon work pants and a gray shirt with an embroidered maroon shield on the chest. Across the shield were stitched the words: SOVEREIGN SERVICE. This was the official uniform of the gas station they owned and operated a mile east of town on Highway 71, which runs south to Storm Lake and north to Sioux Rapids, Spencer, and the Minnesota border beyond. After making the funeral arrangements, Father told Mother and me that Grandfather Tony would be buried in a wine-colored casket, the closest the undertaker could come to the maroon lettering on his workman's heraldry, and so he was.

Mother was careful to save what she thought were the most important of my childhood papers, but my "biography" of Grandfather Tony was lost during one of our many moves following the financial demise of Sovereign Service. I was reminded of this not long ago while reading an interview with John Updike in *The New York Times Book Review*. The novelist whose mother, Linda Grace Hoyer, had recently passed away, was going through her effects and came upon a play he had written in grade school. "I was touched," Updike recalled of this moment, "to realize that she had typed it up, lovingly." Among Updike's earliest memories was the sight of his mother, a long-suffering writer of short stories, at her desk, surrounded by simple equipment: boxes of clean paper, erasers, the brown envelopes that stories would go off in—and come back in. It was not until long after Updike established his literary reputation that his mother began to enjoy some success in her own right. Her desk and the implements of her craft, not her failures, had made all the difference to an attentive son.[1]

When I think back on the literary endeavors of my own childhood some forty years ago, it is surprising how little the tools of the trade have changed. Virtually every one of the thousands of pages I have published were drafted by hand, usually on the yellow legal tablets which I still purchase by the dozen. Being left-handed, I never mastered the godlike swirls and flourishes of the Palmer method of penmanship, let alone the intricacies of the fountain pen, which snagged and blotted to such a degree that it brought me, frustrated, to the verge of tears. On those rare occasions when I was able to forge a readable line or two, there wasn't time for the ink to dry before I smeared it with my trailing hand. Father, who was not known for his sensitivity in such matters, proved unusually solicitous when he learned of my plight. Like Grandfather Tony, he too was left-handed and had endured the even greater indignity of being subjected to classroom ridicule. His teachers had forced him to change hands, unwittingly rendering him ambidextrous in the process.

The simple pencil served me well for years, although the graphite left a dark carbon residue on the edge of my hand that had to be washed off several times a day. The ball point pen proved a great boon, despite the fact that a stubborn ink stain replaced that left by the lead. For one thing, you didn't have to maintain your writing instrument by pausing to sharpen it and thus run the risk of interrupting the creative flow; for another, you didn't have to visit the Hegna's store nearly as often. Indeed, there was a time when a single twenty-cent pen would last half a year or more; if it quit and ink was still visible through the transparent barrel, a subtle coaxing of the brass tip with a lighted match restored the vital flow; that is, until the manufacturer caught on and replaced the brass with plastic, which melts.

Still, I bear certain physical marks that will never

wash away. By the time I entered college, a large, convex callous had formed just below the first joint of my middle finger, where the pressure exerted by untold thousands of pen strokes caused the skin to thicken like a miniature bunion. A similar bump had also formed near the second joint of my little finger, the point at which maximum pressure is exerted on the page. Both have grown larger over the years but I hardly notice, except when I have been away from my desk for awhile and the tissue, having softened from lack of use, remains tender for several days. It is no use trying to relax my hand, as any number of teachers advised me to do. The moment I begin thinking about something else the tension returns, occasionally with such force that the pen literally tears through the manuscript page.

One might suspicion that I have been engaged in a lifelong vendetta agains the typewriter, but such is not the case. I simply grew up in a household without one, and by the time I acquired the skill the dye was long cast. To me, writing is a form of sculpture; a sentence must be molded and remolded any number of times to give it the proper feel and fit. That is something I cannot do on a machine, which moves in one direction only—always forward, never in reverse. I suppose it has to do with the way a writer conceptualizes what he wishes to capture on paper. Few if any of my sentences are preformed, let alone the paragraphs and pages that contain them. On the odd occasion when an insight emerges full-blown, it inevitably vanishes before I can write it out verbatim. Each sentence is a compromise, an approximation of the truth encompassed by means of a crude generalization. This probably means that I am more of a wordsmith than an artist, and the price one pays is measured by the extra blood upon the page.

Until a few months ago, I would rise from my desk and walk over to the corner of my study at the end of a day's writing. There sat my old Remington Quietwriter, its keys laden with the shavings from a hundred erasers, its faded green cover speckled with whiteout, lots of whiteout. I would carry it back to my desk, insert a piece of heavy bond paper, whose thickness just compensated for the badly worn roller, and type up whatever I had written—a few paragraphs, a page, three or four if the gods were exceptionally kind. The ribbon, an endangered species in its own right, was threadbare more often than not, and during the winter months, when the floor was cold, certain keys remained stiff, like the balky legs of reptile at morning light.

There was a time when the typing could have waited until the end of the week, but those days had long passed. So badly has my handwriting deteriorated that even I am unable to decipher it after it is more than a few hours old.

At that point the real editorial process began, scarcely leaving a sentence untouched. Hand-written material added between the lines and in the margins of the page was connected by multicolored arrows and ink trails running every which way, sometimes breaking off and reappearing on the other side. In desperation, illegible printing was substituted for illegible writing, with the predictable result. One long-suffering typist after another deserted the cause, often in the midst of a major campaign. Only by retyping the worst of the worst pages before handing them over was I able to slow the rate of attrition. Lacking both the time and the requisite skill, there was no possibility of completing the final draft myself.

What with the Quietwriter threatening to give up the ghost and my handwriting going on a hundred, it was obvious that something must be done. The reputed virtues of the word processor were not unknown to me. Indeed, I had become fair game among colleagues who,

like the members of a Greek chorus, delighted in exposing one of my many foibles: the historian of science who
stubbornly resists technological change. Even my wife
sided with the Philistines, leaving me little choice: I
went; I saw; I listened to the exuberant young salespeo-
ple; I contemplated the income tax deduction, but I did
not buy—at least not right away. As a matter of fact, I
held out for a not unrespectable three years. Then came
the week before Christmas when the newspaper ad
trumpeted a $500 reduction with no payments until
March. Sweet catharsis—the chorus stilled forever!

Now, when the day's writing is done, I simply swivel
in my desk chair, push a rectangular button labeled
POWER, and insert a small metal disk. Yellow letters
suddenly appear against a black background; a cursor,
defying gravity, dances up and down, forward and back,
at the touch of a key. The long, hand-written page,
which I have clipped to a portable stand, is entered
within minutes, then automatically scanned for spelling
errors. Sentences, nay, whole paragraphs and pages are
moved about at will, added to, subtracted from, formed
and reformed, like so much potter's clay. When all is
well, another button activates a printer that delivers as
many copies as one wishes; no muss, no fuss, no unreadable interlineations, no labyrinth of ink trails, no eraser
shavings, no splotches of whiteout, and, not least, no
typing bill to pay.

Why, then, am I uneasy? Why this melancholy sense
of loss? I glance guiltily at the empty corner where the
old Quietwriter sat and recall the afternoon I put it
away for the last time. It had not been used for weeks
and was fast becoming a dust trap. I placed it in its
battered metal case, and then, before closing the lid,
ran my fingers over the faded letters on the ink-stained
keys. I was startled by their alien, almost primitive, feel,

which is nothing like the silent, electronic keyboard to which I had lately grown accustomed.

It was then that I recalled a contemplative morning spent at the Hemingway house in Key West, Florida, now the haunt of tourists and dozens of half-wild descendants of the novelist's cats. Above the poolhouse, once accessible to the veranda of the main residence by a rope bridge of Hemingway's design, is the study where he wrote some of his finest books, *For Whom the Bell Tolls, Death in the Afternoon, A Farewell To Arms*. What intrigued me most about the room was the old black typewriter at which the grizzled author labored on those increasingly rare mornings when he was able to keep the demon writer's block at bay. Unlike the other period furnishings—the easy chairs, the desk, the lamps, the books and pictures—that typewriter seemed woefully out of place, incapable of producing a single line, let alone several of this century's literary masterpieces. The man who knew its every glitch and idiosyncrasy had departed long since; it would never, indeed could never, be coaxed back to life again.

Although Hemingway used a typewriter, his manuscripts, like those of his contemporaries Faulkner, Steinbeck, and Fitzgerald, often went through several hand-corrected drafts and because of this are invaluable to the literary historian and biographer. They are the writer's equivalent of the preparatory sketches of a da Vinci, a Michelangelo, a Van Gogh. Even more precious are the papers of those who have written in holograph through the centuries. I remember once peering over my wife's shoulder at an illuminated manuscript from the late Middle Ages. In the bottom corner, where some nameless monk had steadied the page with his free-hand, was an ink fingerprint from the century of Petrarch and Dante, Chaucer and Marco Polo. We both reached out in turn and lightly touched the delicate whorls with our own fingertips, while recalling poignant marginalia left by other bored and suffering captives of the scriptorium: "It is time for dinner"; "Wonderful is the robin there singing to us"; "Our cat has escaped from us"; "Alas—my hand!"; "O my breast, Holy Virgin!"

From this time forward, all save the final print-outs of our greatest literary and scientific papers most likely will be lost; indeed, they will have never existed, except as a transitory glow on an illuminated screen. Gone will be the marginal asides of the bored and the witty, the creative doodlings of an Arthur Conan Doyle or a J.R.R. Tolkien, the telltale spot where the pen of an Edgar Allan Poe or a Robert Louis Stevenson hesitated, crossed out, and revised before moving ahead, the false starts and dead ends of a Marie Curie or an Albert Einstein, the profanity of a Luther, the ranting of a Robespierre, the discarded ending of a tragedy by Eugene O'Neill, the droll musings of an Edward Gibbon. Gone will be the thrill of discovery, the joy and wonder of holding the makings of history in one's hand.

Ever more publishers are asking that "manuscripts" be submitted on computer disks whose estimated shelf life is twenty years, far less than that of the millions of moldering volumes printed on acid paper during the past century. And even if the disks were to confound the experts by surviving longer, who can guarantee that archives of the future will possess the technological capacity to retrieve their contents on demand?

I recently read of Robert A. Caro, the biographer and political historian, who has made the saga of Lyndon Johnson his life's work. He has been at it now for over fourteen years and is about to publish the next volume of a projected quartet. The historian works in his Manhattan office at an old desk and makeshift table, surrounded by shelves laden with books relating to his subject. There is no word processor, only an electric portable, making me a technological wizard by comparison. And yet this Merlin has never been offered what could be mistaken for a generous advance, nor has he written two bestsellers or sold his author's rights to the motion picture industry for what his Uncle John, one of the world's great daydreamers, used to call "a blue million."

To be frank, I have never understood how any biographer could devote the lion's share of his career to a single human being, however compelling or important historically. Walking in another person's shoes for four or five years is almost more than I can bear. One learns too little and too much. Moreover the biographer, no less than his subject, changes with time; in looking back, if he is honest with himself, it is certain that he could never write the same book again. How, after two or three decades, can the person he has lived with on such intimate terms not turn into a stranger on the doorstep? Yet it must be admitted that such logic pales when faced with the multivolume masterpieces of a Leon Edel, a William Manchester, a Dumas Malone.

Caro's second home is the Johnson Library in Austin, Texas, repository of a staggering thirty-four million documents. No biographer who hopes to emerge from that great concrete cube alive could possibly be expected to read more than a fraction of its holdings. Like the late Will Durant, Caro is blessed with an Ariel; his wife, Ina, put her own career on hold and moved with her husband to the Hill Country of Texas to labor as his research assistant.[2] Still, the magnitude is staggering, even when divided by two, and leads one to wonder if the biographies of future presidents will have to be written by committees.

Even when the documents from the Johnson collection are added to countless others in archives scattered

across the country, much is lost and will remain so
forever. When Abraham Lincoln wanted to communi-
cate with a member of his cabinet, he either dictated or
penned a letter, had his secretary make a duplicate
copy, and summoned a messenger. When a president
of this century has something urgent on his mind, he
simply picks up the telephone and his words soon vanish
into air. True, a subordinate might scribble some notes
based on the conversation, but such logs are usually
poor substitutes for the written record. And when the
intent is to deceive, as it was during the time of Water-
gate, the cost can be enormous: what would the public,
let alone posterity, have known had it not been for that
forgotten tape recorder?

The slow death of enlightened correspondence, a
phenomenon by no means limited to those in high
office, should be mourned by all society, not just the
biographer. As anyone who has put pen to paper is well
aware, the writer enters a world far removed from that
of the spoken word, a world demanding precision, con-
sonance and, yes, an occasional touch of poetry, however
lackluster. How embarrassed most of us would be if we
were to read the transcript of a three-minute telephone
conversation with a relative or friend: think of the poor
grammar, the sloppy diction, the slang, the sheer vacu-
ity. Recast that same conversation in a letter and it is
mysteriously transformed, likely to be read by the
pleased recipient many times over.

Some candidates for future biographies still write
letters, albeit fewer of them. Even this potential legacy is
seriously threatened, something I discovered only after
purchasing my own word processor. Prior to this, I
would almost always have the department secretary photocopy my correspondence, especially when it was addressed to a fellow scholar or a figure central to my
research. Now I simply print out such letters in my

study, address the envelopes and mail them off, secure in the knowledge that their contents can be called up on the screen at will. The problem is that I am forgetful and often run short of disks. Not wishing to drop everything and drive to the store, I simply erase what seems the least important document on inventory, without first taking the time to print out a copy. Alas, this is inevitably a letter, sometimes two or three.

Consider the consequences if I were a major poet, an elder statesman or a renowned artist. There would always be hope, of course, that the recipient would save the missive, but that, as every biographer knows, is never certain. People travel light these days, moving from state to state the way our grandparents moved across town. There is no room for large attics in the apartments and subdivisions of suburbia, no leatherbound trunks save those in overpriced antique stores. Instead of finding its way into an archive, such a letter could be just as easily thrown in the trash or sold to a private collector, who would no more make its existence known than the suspicious owner of a valuable painting.

I like to think of LUIS—an acronym for Library User Information Systems—as the last of the Bourbons, although he reigns over a much different kingdom than a certain famous ancestor who paid for his sins, both real and imagined, with his head. When LUIS's elevation to the throne was announced by our dean of library services, I broke into a cold sweat and remained edgy for weeks. My anxiety was not without foundation. During the course of my research, I have visited any number of campus libraries whose computer systems left me muttering into my beard, or would have if I had one. In fact, I had recently returned from a long day's trek to a great university some ninety miles from home, an institution whose promotional literature boasts "the third largest research collection in the country." I have no basis for challenging this claim, but I would recommend that an astertisk be inserted, with the caveat: "and the least accessible."

To begin with, there were not enough terminals to go around, forcing me to queue up while two graduate students, apparently husband and wife, attempted to compile the world's most exhaustive bibliography on Byzantium. When my turn finally came, I was greeted by a set of instructions reminiscent of those contained in boxes labeled "some assembly required." No fewer than ten steps were needed to call up a single volume, and even then I was successful only about a third of the time. Finally a long-suffering student, who had been peering anxiously over my shoulder, informed me that some of my queries could not be answered on this terminal, and pointed to another one with an entirely different set of instructions. Unless I planned to be around for some while, she suggested that I look up the works on my list in the discontinued card catalogue. I thanked her for the excellent advice and salvaged what remained of the day.

There was little reason to think that LUIS would prove himself any less imperious. The only consolation was the dean's promise that our card catalogue would be kept up-to-date for an unspecified period, the equivalent, I suspected, of fixing the price of bread to keep the masses from rioting in the streets.

Coronation Day dawned amidst a gray drizzle. Although I had been told ad nauseam that LUIS was "user friendly," I felt not unlike the members of the Third Estate who stood outside in a cold rain at Versailles while Louis XVI welcomed "His clergy" and "His nobility" to the first meeting of the Estates-General in 175 years. My suspicions were not allayed by the simple set of instructions on the terminal screen: "Type in a = (author, last name first); t = (title); s = (subject); then press enter." Vanity of vanities, I typed in a = Christianson, Gale E. Still dubious, I pressed the enter key; within two or three seconds my titles, numbered alphabetically, flashed into view. The instructions at the bottom of the screen commanded me to depress the appropriate key. I pushed number 2 and up came the full catalogue entry for *This Wild Abyss: The Story of the Men Who Made Modern Astronomy*. In addition, LUIS informed me that my book was on loan, an unexpected but welcome bit of news, as well as the date it was due. To return to the full list of books, I was instructed to enter the letter "I" (for index). *Violà*! LUIS had delivered with flawless aplomb.

The procedures for titles and subjects were equally straightforward, but I had my pride. I spent the next half hour probing the system for weaknesses but discovered none. Even the pen and paper in my briefcase had been rendered superfluous. Whether a single title or fifty, the information on the screen was delivered by a printer at the push of another button, and in a fraction of the time it would have taken to write it down. LUIS, a roving staff member proudly volunteered, could even be hooked up to the word processor in my home, placing his millions of obedient subjects at my command. I walked back to my office under a clearing sky, thinking how good it is to be a Frenchman.

Enlightened despot that he is, LUIS, like the other electronic wonders of our age, does not come without a certain cost. Although many authors are loath to admit it, they are secretly anxious to know if their works are being read or they wouldn't have written them in the first place. About a year after my first book was published, a former student wrote to me from one of the booming cities in the Southwest. It had taken several visits to the main library before he was able to obtain a copy of the work. "Your book is very popular," he wrote. "Both sides of the return card are almost filled. They have another copy, and I can only assume that it is in similar demand." Talk about wind in one's sails; I was a hit in Houston!

Yet the time is fast approaching when no author will receive a similar letter of praise again. With LUIS came the electronic check-out. When a book is borrowed, the computer scans the patron's magnetized identification card and prints up a slip of paper containing the due date. Once the volume is returned, the slip is removed from its pocket and discarded by the librarian. The price for this large gain in efficiency is the loss of a tiny bit of history. In the future the only measure of a book's popularity will be an occasional coffee stain and smudged page ends.

This fact was recently brought home to me while I was reading Annie Dillard's autobiography of her youth, *An American Childhood*. The author writes of the 1950s, when her mother regularly drove her to the Homewood Library in the largely black section of Pittsburgh, where she passed many happy hours alternately reading and daydreaming in a great vaulted room with marble floors. The section titled Natural History was among her favorites, and the future author of *Pilgrim at Tinker Creek* fell in love with *The Field Book of Ponds and Streams* by Ann Haven Morgan. The book was "a shocker" from beginning to end, with the greatest shock coming after the fifth grader turned the final page.

> When you checked out a book from the Homewood Library, the librarian wrote your number on the book's card and stamped the due date on a sheet glued to the book's last page. When I checked out *The Field Book of Ponds and Streams* for the second time, I noticed the book's card. It was almost full. There were numbers on both sides. My hearty author and I were not alone in the world,

after all. With us, and sharing our enthusiasm for drag-
onfly larvae and single-celled plants, were, apparently,
many Negro adults.

Who were these people? Had they, in Pittsburgh's
Homewood section, found ponds? Had they found
streams? At home, I read the book again; I studied the
drawings; I reread Chapter 3; then I settled in to study
the due-date slip. People read this book in every season.
Seven or eight people were reading this book every year,
even during the war. . . .

The people of Homewood, some of whom lived in
visible poverty, on crowded streets among burned-out
houses—they dreamed of ponds and streams. They were
saving to buy microscopes. In their bedrooms they fashioned plankton nets. But their hopes were even more in
vain than mine, for I was a child, and anything might
happen; they were adults living in Homewood. There was
neither pond nor stream on the streetcar routes. The
Homewood residents whom I knew had little money and
little free time. The marble floor was beginning to chill
me. It was not fair.[3]

It so happened that I was experiencing a similar
pathos a thousand miles away, only I knew exactly who
the unfulfilled dreamers were. Instead of being assigned a number, everyone who checked out a book
from our small village library wrote his or her name on
the yellow card attached to the inside cover. If the book
was not returned on time, one could expect a phone call
from Lillian Siefken, our eagle-eyed librarian who collected the fine of a penny a day, a consequential sum
when one's allowance was ten cents a week. I paid little
attention to the other names on the cards until the day
I borrowed *Robinson Crusoe* for what must have been the
tenth time. Directly above my signature was the feeble
scrawl of August Rystad, the oldest man in town; indeed,
the oldest man in the world, for all I knew. Old man
Rystad never retired from his hardware business, where

he spent every day but Sunday, from eight in the morning to six in the evening, measuring out three penny nails, cutting tin for guttering, matching rusted screws with new ones, and patiently indulging the young boys of the community, of whom I was one, who spent rainy afternoons examining his small stock of rifles and double-barrel shotguns.

I never viewed the captive hardwareman through the same eyes after my discovery, for, like me, he harbored visions of escaping to a faraway island where the sun burnished your body until it was brown as a buckeye and the palm trees hung heavy with ripening fruit, where there was no schedule to keep save that of your own making, and the rhythmic waves were your only clock. Years later, I came across a line from Dryden's *Absalom and Achitophel* that marked our briefly intersecting lives: "The young men's vision, and the old men's dream."

An old man weary of nails and screws and raucous boys on rainy afternoons was not the only secret dreamer in our midst. Down the block, on the same side of the street as Rystad's Hardware, stood Hegna's Incorporated, a combination grocery and general merchandise store where I bought caps for my toy pistol and inexpensively gaudy vases for my mother on her birthday. Among the various women who clerked there was Mrs. Edwall, a silver-haired widow of aristocratic bearing. She owned the only pear tree and talking parrot in town, either one of which would have qualified her as the resident celebrity. So far as I know, she had never so much as set foot outside Buena Vista county, let alone the state of Iowa. After my illuminating experience with *Robninson Crusoe*, I made it my business to peruse every check-out card I signed. One of my favorite books was a sentimental novel of adolescence titled *Blueberry Mountain*. It was set in Appalachia and told the

story of a youth named Henry and his crippled friend,
both of whom were struggling to keep their impover-
ished families from going under during the depression.
They supplemented their income by picking and selling
the fruit after which the book was titled. The widow
Edwall had also signed the card, and I knew the anticipation she felt when Henry and his friend crossed the
state line for the first time in their rickety automobile.
Too excited to press on, they pulled over to the side of
the road and gingerly set foot on unfamiliar soil, wondering whether it would feel any different than home.
It didn't and I breathed a sigh of relief for the untrav-
eled widow.

One of the most surprising things to me ever written
by a biographer about his craft is this statement from
Leon Edel's *Writing Lives*: "I try to write without consult-
ing my material; this avoids interruption and prevents
me from overloading my text with quotations."[4] I un-
derlined Edel's revelation not once but twice, and then,
for good measure, drew a huge exclamation mark in
the margin next to it. Semester in and semester out, this
quote has never failed to launch some of the liveliest
discussions in my advanced course on biography.

Edel asserts that his method enhances the narrative
flow by protecting it against irrelevancies. The story
must be told in the biographer's words with a directness
that distances the storyteller from the mass and pressure of data. While I agree with Edel in principle, I am
not sufficiently confident of my mental powers to weave
the narrative from unaided memory. Neither, judging
by their comments, are my graduate students. I hold
with those who maintain that irrelevant material can be
deleted at a later time, with the caveat that the biographer, like any writer worthy of the name, must possess
the good sense to do so.

Nor do I subscribe to the methodology acquired by most historians during their student days; namely, that of reducing their notes to 3 by 5 inch cards. Barbara Tuchman writes of toting her note cards around in a shoe box, a practice that enabled her to write her books wherever she might be.

Aside from the fear of misplacing years of hard labor and the intellectual paralysis I associate with unfamiliar surroundings, there would be no way to take my research materials elsewhere, short of a pickup truck or van. And this assuming I had someplace to go. With all due respect to the computer, no invention has had a more revolutionary impact on the working life of the contemporary biographer than the photocopier. For a reasonable fee one can literally walk out of an archive with a facsimile of its holdings in hand.

Such unrestricted access to great quantities of material inevitably produces a glut, or perhaps I should say gluttony. Fearful of overlooking something important, the scholar has a tendency to take home far more than is required, a venial sin to which I have already confessed. Earlier biographers were subject to no such temptation. The constraints imposed by time and manual recording techniques forced them to be far more selective, however much they might have dreamt of gleaning everything.

Still, I am prepared to argue that the advantages of having such a comprehensive body of material at one's disposal far outweigh the drawbacks. To begin with, there is no substitute for accuracy. No matter how committed a researcher may be, the mind inevitably wanders during the tiring process of taking extensive notes, causing the hand to follow. With photocopies available, dates, quotations, and myriad other details can be rechecked as often as need be, thus reducing the number of inadvertent errors that steal into a manuscript.

Then, too, there is the matter of interpretation. The biographer's angle of vision is subject to change: what one sees one day may not be what one sees the next. This is especially true when working with letters, notebooks, and diaries, which usually require several readings. Not only are notes incomplete, unlike primary sources they have a way of growing cold during the months or even years that pass before the biographer returns to them.

But most important of all is the matter of esthetics. Photocopies infuse the creative atmosphere with that quintessential element the Romans called *gravitas*—consequence, dignity, seriousness. They are a constant reminder to the biographer of what he is about, and, because they were generated by his subject, of the responsibility he bears to him. They are the catalysts of inspiration and of musing, the desk-bound voyager's equivalent of Gibbon's arrival in Rome on October 2, 1764: "After a sleepless night I trod with a lofty step the ruins of the Forum; each memorable spot where Romulus *stood*, or Tully spoke, or Caesar fell was at once present to my eye; and several days of intoxication were lost or enjoyed before I could descend to a cool and minute investigation."[5]

I also learned early on that there is much to be gained by reading fine literature while trying to approximate it oneself. The genre is irrelevant: novels and short stories, essays and narrative histories, poetry and plays all serve to deepen one's sensibilities, and by doing so qualify as tools of the trade. Take, for example, Edward Abbey's *Desert Solitaire*, a book published in 1968, but which I only got around to reading while composing this essay some twenty years later, months after Abbey's passing. Standing amidst the canyons and

cliffs of Utah's Arches National Park, Abbey asks himself
the question: "What is the peculiar quality or character
of the desert that distinguishes it, in spiritual appeal,
from other forms of landscape?" His answer, I submit,
could just as well be addressed to the questioning biographer as to shifting sand and mute stone:

> In trying to isolate this peculiarity, if it exists at all and is
> not simply an illusion, we must beware of a danger well
> known to explorers of both the micro- and the macrocos-
> mic—that of confusing the thing observed with the mind
> of the observer, of constructing not a picture of external
> reality but simply a mirror of the thinker. Can this danger
> be avoided without falling into an opposite but related
> error, that of separating too deeply the observer and the
> thing observed, subject and object, and again falsifying
> our view of the world? There is no way out of these
> difficulties—you might as well try running Cataract Can-
> yon without hitting a rock. Best to launch forth boldly,
> with or without life jackets, keep your matches dry and
> pray for the best.

And were my biography of Loren Eiseley not already at
the printers, I would have appropriated this from Abbey, for nothing in all the 500 pages on my subject is
more apt:

> I discovered that I was not opposed to mankind but only
> to man-centeredness, anthropocentricity, the opinion
> that the world exists solely for the sake of man; not to
> science; which means simply knowledge, but to science
> misapplied, to the worship of technique and technology,
> and to that perversion of science properly called scien-
> tism; and not to civilization but to culture.[6]

Musings on vanished library cards and the largely
forgotten people who signed them might never have
resurfaced were it not for my chance reading of a little
girl's love for *The Field Book of Ponds and Streams*, for

surely memories are one of the most important tools of the biographer's trade. John Updike's evocation of his writer-mother is too poignant to forget. So, too, this line from George Orwell's *1984*, which I copied and saved for future use: "It was as though the surface of the glass had been the arch of the sky, enclosing a tiny world with its atmosphere complete." All the while I was growing up, such an object occupied a special place on the spinet in my grandparents' living room. When the angle of the afternoon sun was just right, the ceiling directly over-head came alive with the magnified spectrum of re-fracted light, as beautiful as anything I would see until I entered my first cathedral. The paperweight, Grand-mother often told me, had belonged to Grandfather Tony, who had purchased it long before they were married. He had actually seen it made in a glassworks whose name and location she could no longer remem-ber. This tiny world now sits atop my study shelf; I occasionally reach out and take it in the palm of my hand. Peering down through the transparent atmo-sphere like an aging god, I see the speck of earth where Grandfather and I last hunted nightcrawlers together, the little pond where we threw the sunfish back but kept the bullheads, the Sovereign Service emblem, the rust-ing Willy—and, far away on the horizon, the shimmer-ing blue expanse that will one day carry me back to my ancestral home on the fjord.

9

"Writing Lives Is the Devil!"

It has always seemed to me that the novelist and short story writer reap all the sympathy when, for no apparent reason, the ink suddenly stops flowing. "I suffer stylistic abscesses; and sentences keep itching without coming to a head," Gustave Flaubert wrote his understanding mistress, Louise Colet, in October 1851, as he was beginning his most famous work, *Madame Bovary*. "I am fretting, scratching. What a heavy oar the pen is, and what a strong current ideas are to row in!" Two weeks later, in another letter to Colet, Flaubert's anguish reasserted itself: "I spoil a considerable quantity of paper. So many deletions! Sentences are very slow in coming. What a devilish style I have adopted! A curse on simple subjects!"[1]

And what about Tom Wolfe whose *Bonfire of the Vanities* has sold a million, or is it three? When the words will not come the good author simply makes an appointment with his tailor to be fitted for a new suit. "The nice thing about custom-made clothes is that they take over. You can have four or five fittings, and the tailor shops are usually nice places to hang out." The best is yet to be. Not only does the author maintain his reputation for sartorial splendor, he has put himself in the proper mental frame to produce yet another best-seller: "The suit is so expensive that you have to write something eventually to pay the bill."[2] Crackle on, O Bonfire, crackle on!

For those of us in slightly more straitened circumstances, one victim of writer's block has offered the following suggestions. Keep a scrapbook containing all of your acceptance slips, check vouchers, fan letters, and "other cheery memorabilia." Should you possess that rarest of documents, a complimentary letter from an editor, put it right up front, the theory being that what you have done before you can do again. If this proves ineffectual you should become more aggressive: "Go for a walk and take a notebook and pencil with you." If all else fails, try writing greeting cards.[3]

While I appreciate the advice, my blockages tend to resemble boulders more than peas.

The angst is all the more acute when one is a writer of nonfiction, that terribly awkward term without synonym. Whereas the "blocked" novelist is surrounded by a galaxy of comforting lights—Faulkner, Hemingway, Capote, Hellman, Mailer—the becalmed "realtor," as someone once called the historian and biographer, finds himself staring into the literary equivalent of a black hole.

True, the great historian of the American frontier, Francis Parkman, is said to have written only six lines a day. Yet he did so in the not unrespectable time of fifteen minutes, an indication that a chronic nervous affliction and extreme weakness of sight were more to blame than Clio, that notoriously fickle Muse. The Trappist monk Thomas Merton, one of the most prolific writers of the fifties and sixties, claimed to have experienced intellectual paralysis while writing his first purely theological work, a great synthesis on the internal life drawn from Scripture and the Fathers of the Church. While there is no reason to doubt Merton's word, some things remain relative, even within the sanctity of a whitewashed cell. With only two hours a day to practice his craft, Merton would write as many as fifty pages a week, tear them up, and begin again. Though he wrote his editor, Naomi Burton, of "a block," the problem, ironically, seems to have been one of surfeit rather than famine: "I only lose the freshness of the original and am just as prolix over again, but in a different and duller way."[4]

For me, only one author of nonfiction has truly captured the moment of abject terror when the red light flashes on and the literary oil ceases to flow. While working on a chapter of *The Proud Tower* chronicling the Dreyfus Affair, Barbara Tuchman watched helplessly while her writing slowed to a trickle, and then "One dreadful day . . . I went into my study at nine and stayed there in a blank coma until five, when I emerged without having written a single word. Anyone who is a writer will know how frightening that was. You feel you have come to the end of your powers; you will not finish the book; you may never write again."[5]

I suspect the reason why so few biographers are willing to discuss this syndrome publicly is due to a sense of personal embarrassment. The historian's first duty, as each of us quickly learns, is to obtain as much *factual* knowledge about his subject as possible. Accumulate sufficient material and the facts will in turn determine how the past should be explained or interpreted. Auguste Comte, the nineteenth-century social reformer and founder of the philosophical school known as Positivism, even went so far as to claim that historians would in due course uncover the "laws" of historical development. Although one hears few such grandiose declarations these days, the belief abides that if the research is done well the story will virtually write itself. Thus, why should a competent historian get stuck when his file cabinets are bulging and his desk is awash with papers gathered from over half of creation?

In Tuchman's case the blockage resulted from the difficult task of selection. The author was attempting to pack the entire Dreyfus Affair into a score of pages, yet at the same time provide the uninitiated reader with enough information to enable him to grasp what was going on, and this while not talking down to her peers, who would inevitably review the book. Faced with selecting and sifting on one level, with synthesizing and forging the narrative on another, the mind of the historian seized in panic: "You may never write again!"

More daunting still is the moment when the biographer must call a halt to his archival labors and take pen in hand, perhaps after a haitus of several years. Seated at his desk, with a ream of blank pages just visible out of the corner of his eye, he must begin somehow. But where? Even the battle-hardened Leon Edel has quivered when faced with the moment of truth:

> How in that material amid the multitudinous months and days of another's life, is he to find those points of departure which will enable him to proceed? In his mind a million facts exert simultaneous pressure; around him are notes and files which now must be converted into a readable book; and all this crowded detail must flow in a narrative, calm and measured and judicial, capable of capturing a reader and conveying in some degree the intensity which has kept the biographer for long months at his task.[6]

Saturated with documents, the biographer has become a bondsman, longing for the literary freedom accorded the novelist.

How wonderful it would be, he fantasizes when lost in the pathless wood of archival minutiae, to be able to do what Truman Capote, E. L. Doctorow, and Norman

Mailer have done. Begin by selecting a series of gripping historical or contemporary events, create a supporting cast of oddball characters to further whet the reader's appetite, supply them with convincing (albeit fictional) dialogue, and then rearrange the material so as to achieve a perfectly balanced structure. Behold! *In Cold Blood, Ragtime, Armies of the Night,* a genre for which Doctorow has coined the clever term "faction," an intoxicating blend of fact and fiction, which, the novelist contends, is really the way each of us comes to grips with the past.

Doctorow may well be right, but that is beside the point. The biographer, like every other historian, has no business deliberately crossing the line, or even attempting to blur it. Moreover, Capote's haunting psychological dance with two mass murderers—the work which supposedly started it all—was a Johnny-come-lately by upwards of 2,500 years. Herodotus, the "Father of History," circled most of the Mediterranean on foot, taking notes and asking questions of anyone who would talk to him. Thucydides, younger by a generation, employed similar techniques when writing his incomparable *History of the Peloponnesian War,* the outstanding feature of which is the funeral oration of Pericles, the most eloquent Memorial Day speech ever given. Some two millennia later James Boswell, the dauntless, social-climbing Scot, dusted off this ancient methodology and used it to write what many contend is the finest biography of all.

Doubtless the reason the pseudohistorical approach is so compelling to the novelist is that it provides a ready-made structure, thus easing the pressure to create one's own from scratch. History, after all, is full of great stories, many far more interesting than those spun purely from imagination. What mind could have dreamt up Julius Caesar, Elizabeth I, Shakespeare, or Jesus of

Nazareth, Sitting Bull, Sojourner Truth, Rasputin, or Winston Churchill? This is the historian's advantage at the outset, and no one can blame the novelist for wishing to narrow the handicap before entering the fray. On the other hand, as an artist under oath the historian is never free to falsify a quote, to alter the appearance of a character or a setting, to disregard an important piece of evidence simply because it doesn't seem to fit. The narrative is his art, the footnote his science, and the two must always reinforce and validate each other.

Every human being, especially the writer, should have a private refuge from which all others are excluded. As a child growing up in a tiny Iowa village, I often hid away in a ramshackle shed at the back of my parents' house. There I lay on a comforting pile of old corncobs, watching motes of dust ascend golden columns of autumn light. I did not know it then, but I was beginning to develop the luxuriant sense of self that comes from monitoring one's inner weather. With the onset of adolescence came the need for greater distance. I began walking out into the countryside to the banks of a meandering stream, a place of green enchantment soon left behind when we moved to a city far away. Nature yielded to art during my graduate studies in Pittsburgh. When the life of the mind grew tedious, I would retreat to The Carnegie Museum of Art and lose myself for hours in the pink ponds and vibrant flowers of Monet, the mesmerizing vortices and undulating orchards of Van Gogh. I always knew that others experienced a similar need, but it was not until I read mythographer Joseph Campbell that I fully understood its universal significance:

> You must have a room, or a certain hour or so a day, where you don't know what was in the newspapers that

morning, you don't know who your friends are, you don't know what you owe anybody, you don't know what anybody owes to you. This is a place where you can simply experience and bring forth what you are and what you might be. This is the place of creative incubation. At first you may find that nothing happens there. But if you have a sacred place and use it, something eventually will happen.[7]

Ever since donning the guise of a university professor, my private refuge has been the stereotypic book-lined study, disheveled and a bit dusty about the edges. Within its confines I have experienced many days of the kind described by Barbara Tuchman, but always, as Campbell promised, something eventually happened— or at least it did until that terrible summer not so very long ago.

I was approaching the midpoint of my biography of Isaac Newton and had just finished a chapter titled "A Pitfall in Eden," chronicling my subject's bitter intellectual confrontation with the pitiable Robert Hooke, an experimental genius destined always to stand in Newton's shadow. Before me, like a cloud enshrouded Everest, loomed the chapter on the *Principia mathematica*, easily the most important of the book. I had already selected what I thought was an excellent title, "The Most Perfect Mechanic of All," and found in *Bartlett's* the epigraph I had long been searching for, drawn from the journal of the Swiss Professor Henri-Frederic Amiel: "Doing easily what others find difficult is talent; doing what is impossible for talent is genius." Now all I had to do was write the thing.

The first two sections, containing mostly background material, went smoothly enough; it was on reaching the third that the pen locked in my hand. How to translate the abstract concepts and mathematical propositions of our greatest book of science into the

vernacular of the educated layperson? How to commu-
nicate grandeur without resorting to purple prose? How
to compass genius while possessing none of it onself?
The words of Newton's publisher, Edmond Halley, who
was blessed by fate in his own right, began stalking me
like a malevolent ghost: "Nearer to the gods no mortal
may approach."[8]

Each evening at dusk my spirits faded, knowing that
in a mere twelve hours I would be back at my desk
seeking the breakthrough common sense told me must
come. I slept fitfully while promising scenarios danced
around the edge of consciousness, only to dissolve like
vapor at morning light. The July heat and humidity
were also taking their toll. Lacking air conditioning, I
tried a tactic John Cheever employed while still an
unknown novelist writing in the stifling confines of a
New York City apartment during the dog days of August; namely, stripping down to my underwear and
training a fan on my backside. The prickly heat retreated but the pen refused to advance. I even thought
of junking the desk on which everything I had published was written. Once the property of a man who
committed suicide, there was a possibility that either it
or the chair in which I sat daily for eight tortuous hours
was haunted.

Most experienced writers will tell you that when you
have reached this stage one would be well advised to
take a break and turn to other things. In quest of both
inspiration and release, I attempted to compromise by
quitting a few minutes earlier each afternoon. Seemingly aimless drives down winding country roads helped
a little until I realized that, no matter the direction from
which I started, I almost always wound up at the same
location. I would park near a chocolate-colored river
and walk up the bank to the site of a dam built by some
long-forgotten miller in the middle of the last century.

Nothing of the mill itself remained, save the masonry outlines of the crumbling foundation. A few feet away, turned on its side and half buried in the earth, lay the massive silica and flint grinding wheel, its once-grooved surface smoothed by a million revolutions, then burnished to a gleaming white by alternating cycles of wind and weather. As summer wore on and rain became scarce, the water clearing the dam slowed to a rivulet; even nature seemed to be mocking my barren state.

While musing amidst these nineteenth-century ruins, I suddenly remembered a short story by Stephen Vincent Benét from my grade school days, when reading was still the national pastime, at least while the baseball diamond lay frozen solid beneath a sea of drifted snow. "The Devil and Daniel Webster" begins as a "yarn they tell in the border country, where Massachusetts joins Vermont and New Hampshire."[9]

Farmer Jabez Stone, around whose fate the tale unfolds, was not so much a bad man as an unlucky one. If Jabez planted corn, he harvested insects; if he sowed potatoes, he reaped blight; if stones cropped up in a neighbor's field, boulders materialized in his. He once traded a lame horse for one with the staggers and even gave something extra in the bargain. Finally one day Jabez got so fed up with his lot while plowing rock in the north forty that he cried out in desperation: "I vow it's enough to make a man want to sell his soul to the Devil! And I would, too, for two cents!" The very next day, around suppertime, a soft-spoken stranger in a dark suit drove up the lane in a handsome buggy and asked to see the man who had summoned him. It took only minutes to draw up the infernal pact, which, after all, was pretty much your standard document. Seven happy and prosperous years and then the mortgage would come due. Jabez Stone pricked his finger with a silver pin and signed on the dotted line.

Sitting there in solitude on the great millstone, I began to weigh the possibilities. I knew that Jabez Stone, after growing rich and respectable, had been spared at the last moment by the herculean oratory of Daniel Webster, but I also realized the chances were slight that anyone with similar powers would speak on my behalf, providing the need should arise. On the other hand, I was asking for very little when measured against the cupidity of the Faustian ego: neither wealth nor universal knowledge, power nor fame, physical beauty nor a sip from the fountain of youth. All I needed was a brief artistic collaboration on a *single* chapter of manuscript, far less, I suspicioned, than a certain prominent author who was very much on my mind.

The person in question had recently appeared on a television talk show whose host, like everyone else in the audience, was astounded by his literary output—a staggering 400 or so volumes of fiction and nonfiction already in print and, judging by the tenor of the conversation, at least another hundred to follow. How could anyone, I kept asking myself, turn out the equivalent of a book and a half a month? When did he do his research and edit his manuscripts, let alone proofread an unending river of galleys before going to press? Indeed, when did he find time to negotiate with multiple publishers (no single house could possibly handle the volume), let alone scrutinize the fine print in the scores of contracts? I was reminded of the Marquis de l'Hopital's query concerning Newton: "[D]oes he eat and drink and sleep; is he like other men?"[10] Yet there this fellow sat, self-confident and clear-eyed, seemingly unawed by his accomplishments and planning no respite on the road to literary immortality. It was at this point that I began to rethink my position on the conspiracy theory of history.

If, like Jabez Stone, he was being aided by a preternatural hand, the scale was such that it must belong to none other than the Son of the Morning Star. The trick would be to win old Lucifer over to my cause, preferably without paying the supreme price.

My problem was compounded by the fact that I knew virtually nothing of the occult, and had no real inclination to learn. Besides, drawing a pentagram in the back yard is almost guaranteed to arouse suspicion among the neighbors. I had no acquaintance with witches either—at least none that I knew of—so that wrangling an invitation to a sabbat also seemed out of the question. And even had that been possible, I doubted that I could abide the despicable agenda: dancing naked to the sound of macabre music made with human bones; kissing a goat or a toad in homage; throwing oneself into promiscuous sexual orgies before settling down to feast on such delicacies as fricasees of bats and mice. Preferring to keep a low profile and maintain some sense of decorum, I privately and silently declared myself open for business, then settled down to await further developments.

In the anxious days that followed, I sometimes sniffed an unfamiliar odor in the air, perhaps sulfuric, but I couldn't be sure. Every time the doorbell rang, especially around the dinner hour, I half expected to be greeted by the dark-suited stranger whose pointed white teeth had caused Jabez Stone's dog to run away howling, with his tail between his legs. At evening I occasionally snapped to attention at my desk, sensing something latent and lurking in the shadowed corridor beyond. To my already fretful sleep was added a further complication. Whenever I awoke, I sat bolt upright and squinted into the glow cast by a distant streetlight, searching for the telltale outline of the "great, dark, bearded one" of Dante's recurring dream.

Meanwhile, the words were coming back, at first in dribs and drabs, then in sentences, and finally whole paragraphs that added up to pages! The Devil, it seemed, had found me wanting, and I was angry at not being offered some sort of contract. Without realizing it at the time, I had put my ire to good use by turning it on Newton, who came hurtling down from Everest with a thud. Who did he think he was, anyway, making a shambles of my life when I had paid him the supreme compliment of devoting five years of it to his? So what if he was a genius and I but a plodding scholar; even biographers are entitled to their feelings.

And so it was that time had proven Joseph Campbell right. While the Devil never showed his smiling face in Terre Haute, something had happened after all, even if it was at a cost approximating Hell.

The too-painful memory of that summer has kept me from returning to my quiet place beside the chocolate-colored river. Still, I expect to be writing another biography soon, and I already have designs on a little gazebo within walking distance of my home. The weathered boards are smooth to the touch, the surrounding oaks alive with birds and squirrels and, during the dog days of August, the soporific drone of amatory cicadas.

The novelist Virginia Woolf once tried her hand at literary biography; after great difficulty she finally produced a slender volume on the artist and critic Roger Fry. "Dear me, I'm so tired of correcting Roger, and it's so bad," Woolf wrote despairingly of the manuscript to Vita Sackville-West. "How can one make a life out of six cardboard boxes full of tailor's bills, love letters and old picture postcards?" The frustrated biographer expressed herself even more succinctly to Vanessa Bell: "Yes, writing lives is the devil!"[11]

10

Arrows in the Blue

Other than Sunday school, which I attended faithfully from the time I was in the womb, I had no experience with formal education until first grade, there being no kindergarten in Rembrandt, Iowa. My father went off to war on the very day of my birth, but an aptitude for electronics kept Sergeant Christianson stateside, where he spent the better part of four years moving from one military base to another, safe but anxious while his friends stormed the beaches of Anzio or, like his handsome younger brother, flew missions over "the Hump." My mother and I lived with her parents on their sprawling farm with the kind of giant red barn that is fast disappearing in the Midwest. It was there, with the help of my Grandmother Jesse and several doting aunts, that she taught me the alphabet. I was soon picking out one-syllable words from the local newspaper that "Old Harry" deposited in my grandparents' mail box through the window of a rusty Model T. A bit later my well-worn storybooks—*Treasure Island, Uncle Remus, The Brothers Grimm*—began yielding up their delicious secrets without adult assistance.

My mother, a spirited but prudent woman, would surely have kept her son unlettered had she any inkling of the trouble in store for both of us. Aside from being slow-witted or incorrigible, nothing in those days ranked so high on the educator's list of deadly sins as the child who could read before entering the classroom. This was insubordination, pure and simple, a subversion of the school's sacred duty. The damage inflicted might never be repaired; besides, how was a teacher to cope if even one of her charges failed to march in rank at the outset?

I have never forgotten the day when my classmates and I were issued our first readers. My spirits soared despite a stern lecture by Miss Wagner on the horrors that awaited should any damage befall a single page of the taxpayers' property. We then formed a line and filed past her desk, while she duly recorded our names and the condition of the books entrusted to our care. Only then, with a glare befitting an Oriental potentate, did Miss Wagner relinquish the red-covered treasure. I half ran back to my seat, eager to begin turning the pages.

The title of the little work has faded from memory, but it was one of the ubiquitous Dick and Jane series which dominated elementary classrooms for a generation. Having been at the front of the line (everything in grade school was done alphabetically), I finished what was supposed to be an entire semester's work in the time it took the others to claim their readers. Yet, as instructed, I carried the book home that evening to "familiarize" myself with the pictures and promptly committed the inane contents to memory. "Look, Dick, look. Look. Look. Look. See Spot run. Run. Run. Run." By the end of the week I was giving impromptu recitations to my awed classmates during recess and even repeated my performance when egged on by a fellow miscreant during Sunday school class.

Now Rembrandt, as you may have guessed, is a very small town, and this smart alecky behavior did not go unnoticed. I soon found myself in the principal's office after a humiliating dressing-down by Miss Wagner in front of the tittering class. My mother was called in and she too was reprimanded for meddling in the educational process. It was to be understood that her son would receive no special attention and that he must participate in the same reading exercises as his classmates. Furthermore, I would be watched closely for any signs that my premature literacy had damaged my aptitude for learning.

Painful though it was, the experience of being scolded for reading only reinforced my love of books. While waiting for the others to catch up, I endured the boredom by paying frequent visits to the school library on the Jovian third floor, where the sophomores, juniors, and seniors took their classes. Many of the books were badly out of date and most defied my powers of comprehension, but that mattered little, especially when the titles conveyed a sense of the exotic.

Then came the day when I happened on a book by the writer with the perfect name, Jack London. The gilt lettering on the faded spine instantly captured a youth's romantic heart: *The Call of the Wild*. The brief Table of Contents bespoke volumes: "Into the Primitive," "The Law of Club and Fang," "The Dominant Primordial Beast," which sent me scurrying to the ponderous Webster's Dictionary on the oak pedestal nearby. I soon learned that the literary sire of Buck had also fathered *White Fang*, whose chapter titles were equally thrilling: "The Wall of the World," "The Law of Meat," "The Makers of Fire," "The Trail of the Gods."

There is no need to recount the details of my resulting daydreams; suffice it to say that their disclosure would have strengthened Miss Wagner's case against the child too early taught to read.

Later on in grade school, as our study of language grew more complex, I found that Jack London had affected me in quite another way. Before being permitted to write a paper of any length, we were required to draft an outline. One could never have an A without a

B, and any student who hoped to earn more than a "C"
for his efforts was well advised to foray much deeper
into the alphabet. This seemed to me a great waste of
time, something Jack London would never have been
caught dead doing. Moreover, I was no good at it. How
did you know for certain what you were going to say
until you were at the point of saying it? Instead, I
compiled a mental list of the most important points I
thought I wanted to make, then composed my paper
accordingly. The problem was that the outline always
came due in advance of the final product, forcing me to
write in haste so that I could construct the hated document from the prose. Indeed, I have worked this way
ever since, the formal outline now a distant but still
unpleasant memory.

The books that left the deepest impression on me
always seemed to be those with the most arresting titles,
what one of my finest teachers referred to as "grab-
bers": Hawthorne's foreboding *The Scarlet Letter*, Twain's
deceptively whimsical *Huckleberry Finn*, Dickens' en-
grossing albeit historically flawed *A Tale of Two Cities*,
Defoe's escapist *Robinson Crusoe*. Who was Moby-Dick? I
wondered and still do, after having repeated to myself
American literature's greatest opening line—a mere
three words—more times than I can count. Yet it was
not until I became an undergraduate that I discovered
another writer who could hold his own as a titlist with
the great Jack London.

Like London, the Hungarian-born Arthur Koestler
was a restless intellectual, a natural adventurer drawn to
the principles of Communism as a young man during
the global depression of the early thirties. While covering the Spanish Civil War for an English newspaper in
1937, Koestler was captured by the Fascists and sen-
tenced to death, an experience chronicled in *Spanish
Testament*. After his release through British intervention,

he went to France, where he was arrested by the invading Germans and put in a concentration camp at Le Vernet, about which he wrote in *Scum of the Earth*. But it was the Soviet purge trials of old Bolsheviks that provided the grist for his best known novel, *Darkness at Noon*, which exposed the sunless side of Stalin's granite face. The work so affected me, both emotionally and intellectually, that I still assign it to my class in Modern World Civilization.

Yet it's as a biographer I find Koestler at his most interesting. *The Sleepwalkers*, my favorite among several provocative works, is a philosophical and biographical history of astronomy that covers much of the same ground as would my own first book. As always Koestler leaves no doubt about where he stands, beginning with his choice of titles, which he explicates in the Preface: "The history of cosmic theories . . . may without exaggeration be called a history of collective obsessions and controlled schizophrenias; and the manner in which some of the most important individual discoveries were arrived at reminds one more of a sleepwalker's performance than an electronic brain's."[1] While there is much in this statement to ponder and debate, the Table of Contents alone is filled with more arrows in the blue than many an entire volume. Part one, "The Heroic Age," was a time of "Ionian Fever," " 'Soft Stillness and the Night,' " "The Rise of the Circular Dogma," and "The Cubist Universe." In Part Two, titled "Dark Interlude," one is introduced to the medieval Christian vision of the cosmos via "The City of God," "The Earth as a Tabernacle," and "The Age of Double-Think." Nicolas Copernicus is "The Mystifier" who does not put in an appearance until page 119, where he is pictured on his deathbed, too far gone to recognize the first copy of *De revolutionibus* just arrived from the printer's. A tortured Johannes Kepler, the first lawgiver and true hero of the book, is diagnosed as suffering from "emotional hemo-philia" in a section grandiosely titled "Orphic Purge," as a victim of "The Gravity of Fate" in another. Galileo, telescope in hand, creates a "Lunar Nightmare" while Isaac Newton, the grand synthesizer, rends the history of thought by casting gravity across the void—" 'Tis all in Pieces" à la John Donne. In the face of such verve, how could the prospective reader fail to be drawn in?

Inspired by Koestler and by Lewis Mumford, an-other of my intellectual heroes, I followed suit by com-posing subtitles for the chapters of my first work. For example, "Johannes Kepler: The Mystical Lawgiver" was parceled into "The Misfit," "Passions of the Heart and Mind," "A Meeting of Giants," "The Lawgiver," "Before the Storm," "Season of the Witch," and "Harmony from Chaos." Apart from the hope of gaining a wider audi-ence, the exercise helped sustain the creative process. Every few pages I looked forward to the composition of another rubric, a challenge to one's esthetic sense as well as a respite on a long and lonely pilgrimage of self-flagellation. Many beginnings and endings, minichap-ters within chapters gave me the chance to switch course in midstream or to change historical time zones without impinging upon the narrative—to keep the reader, in the words of biographer Catherine Drinker Bowen, turning the page.

As historians are wont to point out, every gain has its cost. I fell victim by degrees to the incurable malady of "Titular Obsession," so named by an anonymous headline writer for *The New York Times Book Review*. I was researching my biography of Loren Eiseley when I came across a brief interview with Eiseley's fellow Ne-braskan and close friend, Wright Morris. "Loren and I would spend hours trying to get the right titles for our next books. It even got to be such an obsession that I once got him on the phone at 2 in the morning and said, 'Listen to this one.'" After Morris relayed his brainstorm, there was a long pause. "It sounds good," Eiseley finally replied, "but how about if I let you know after I wake up?" The work in question told the story of Morris's father's ill-starred venture as a chicken farmer and was eventually titled *The Works of Love*. Eiseley was rewarded for his loss of sleep when he turned the title page to find his name, along with that of Sherwood Anderson, in the dedication.

When I later interviewed Morris for the biography, he confirmed what I had read in the *Book Review*. Speculating about titles "was one of our indoor substitutes for double-crosstics and charades." Eiseley inclined toward what Morris termed the "comprehensive metaphysical title. He wanted to get that type exactly appropriate to his nature—something that would include everything and still have the poetic resonance. Both of us might go overboard a bit on one aspect or another, whatever it [was] we were attempting to state."[2]

Eiseley's handwritten manuscripts provided eloquent supporting testimony. An article titled "The Snout," which appeared in the September 1950 issue of *Harper's*, had undergone at least nine title changes, ranging from "The Appearances," "The Crawlers," "The Quagmire," and "A Strange Door," to "A Place of Low Life," "The Door in the Bog," "The Mud Skippers," and "Things to be Watched."[3] It is a tribute to his sensitivity that, almost without exception, the evolutionary process was for the better.

It is said that Hemingway, another hopeless addict, had thirty titles in reserve should Maxwell Perkins, his editor at Scribner's, veto "For Whom the Bell Tolls." Although Eiseley's back-up list was never as long as Papa's, there were times when he expended more effort titling a work than finishing it. In 1948 an unwritten agreement had been struck with Harper and Brothers to publish a volume of his essays. "*Manhunt* is a much better title than any we had thought of," Jack Fischer, his editor, wrote him in July.[4] While Harper's continued to publish Eiseley's essays at a steady pace, little was heard of the proposed book for another four years. Finally, in December 1952, Eiseley wrote to report that he had hit upon "a good scheme. It will demand, however, a much different title than our old one, *Manhunt*." He had been reading St. Augustine and was captivated by the theologian's metaphor: "Man himself is a great deep."[5] The avuncular Fischer pronounced *The Great Deep* excellent, provided a subtitle could be found to distinguish the work from that of Rachel Carson. "I should be very eager," Fischer added, "to see the complete first draft."[6]

Three years later, his manuscript not yet finished, Eiseley broke ranks with Harper's and signed a contract with Random House. In a September 1956 letter to his new editor, Hiram Haydn, he mentioned "toying" with the idea of changing the title to *Bones and Searches* on the grounds that it seems "less pretentious." Of course, *The Dark Side of the Planet*, *The Crack in the Absolute*, and *The Night Tide* were not without their charms. A month later, author and editor compromised on *The Crack in the Absolute*, allowing a beleagured Wright Morris to breathe a little easier. The 200-page manuscript, some eight years in the making, was personally delivered by Eiseley on November 13. In a follow-up letter the author confessed that the question of the title was nagging him still. He wondered if *The Crack in the Absolute* sounded "too weightily philosophical" and thus ran the risk of missing the "nature public."[7] Two weeks later, while scanning the journal of the Swiss professor and critic Henri-Frederic Amiel, he found what he was looking for: "It is as though the humanity of our day, had, like the migrating birds, an immense journey to make across space." Eiseley's only regret was that *The Immense Journey* would have been the perfect title for his own autobiography, which was yet to be written. But just in case Haydn had any doubts, *The Judgment of the Birds*, *Tracks in the Night*, and *From What Star*, the latter drawn from Edmund Blunden's poem about a puff ball, were also very tantalizing.[8]

The transition from narrative history to biography had deprived me of the luxury of composing subtitles. All was not lost, however, for I followed my established pattern of dividing each chapter into sections, substituting Roman numerals for what would have seemed overly pretentious rubrics. Still, I was nagged by a sense of creative loss—by the prohibition against nudging my wife in the small hours and whispering, "What do you think about this one?" Luckily, a solution to my predicament suddenly manifested itself with the arrival in the mail of Edmund Morris's Pulitzer Prize-winning biography, *The Rise of Theodore Roosevelt*. Morris cleverly begins each of his twenty-eight chapters with a quote from T.R.'s favorite epic poem, *The Saga of King Olaf*, by Longfellow. So too the epilogue chronicling the fall of President William McKinley to an assassin's bullet and the fulfillment of Roosevelt's ascent to power:

> *A strain of music closed the tale,*
> *A low monotonous, funeral wail*
> *That with its cadence wild and sweet,*
> *Made the long Saga more complete.*

Within the hour I was in my car headed for the nearest bookstore, where I began my quest for perfect epigraphs with the purchase of *Bartlett's Familiar Quotations*, fifteenth edition.

Anyone who begins to look up a word in a dictionary and is distracted by the etymology of five others will have known the pleasure I experienced. *Bartlett's* fifteen hundred-odd pages were soon interleaved with scores of markers torn from the corners of newspapers, magazine covers, letters from friends, and, in an occasional act of desperation, my classroom lecture notes: multiple epigraphs for chapters already written, for those not yet begun, for books in the state aboriginals call "the dream time." For Newton's birth I chose Shakespeare, the only countryman whose genius compared with my subject's: "A star danced, and under that I was born." For his early manhood, the redoubtable Samuel Johnson: "Towering in the confidence of twenty-one." Contemporary John Dryden spoke for the chapter tracing the early prism experiments, the formulation of the calculus, and the first intimations of universal gravitation: "The young men's vision, and the old men's dream." And so it went; twenty-one chapters, twenty-one epigraphs, the final one drawn from the melancholy physician Sir Thomas Browne, who, like Newton, struggled to reconcile science and religion: "The created world is but a small parenthesis in eternity." It was almost as if, by quoting from their works, the great minds of the past were bestowing their collective benediction on mine. Nor was I unaware of the fact that "epigraphing" would make me appear more knowledgeable in the eyes of many readers than is actually the case.

To my chagrin, my normally congenial editor dug in her heels when the manuscript crossed her desk. "Why do you need epigraphs," she protested over the telephone, "when your chapters tell the tale well enough?"

"I am pleased that you think so," I replied, "but epigraphs provide a sense of focus at the outset. Besides, they add a touch of elegance, don't you think?"

The heavy silence on the other end of the line tempted me to quote from a concilatory letter Max

Perkins sent to Thomas Wolfe, in January 1937: "I believe the writer . . . should always be the final judge, and I meant you to be so. I have always held to that position and have sometimes seen books hurt thereby, but at least as often helped. The book belongs to the author."[9] However, not wishing to damage my case by appearing smug, I held my tongue and switched tactics by ticking off a list of best-selling biographers who employ the epigraph. "And think of the browser who spends only a minute or two deciding whether to buy a book or return it to the shelf. Your very argument that the epigraph encapsulates the chapter's main theme becomes a selling point. Besides, Isaac Newton is a daunting subject; we want to attract literary buffs as well as students of science."

"I'll think about it," was her guarded response. A month later, when the copyedited manuscript was returned to me for a final reading, the epigraphs remained untouched.

In addition to marking up a manuscript, editors are fond of attaching little "flags" to the page margins—yellow, blue, or green rectangles of paper containing brief and often cryptic queries to be addressed by the author. The more flags, the blacker one's mood, especially when a chapter title is called into question. I quote directly from one such cheery banner: "Suggest you rethink title. Too trite in this context." And from another: "Suggest you rethink title. Difficult to connect this with character/time of chapter."

When this happens the problem is compounded for an author such as myself, who is fond of secreting the title somewhere in the chapter, as in this essay, which also happens to be the title of Arthur Koestler's first volume of autobiography. After some deliberation, I detached this upsetting marginalia and tossed it in a desk drawer to await final disposal when the coast

cleared. I have done this several times since and have
never been caught out, doubtless because an overbur-
dened editor has nothing tangible to remind him of his
mischief. I might add that the practice works equally
well when addressing other supercilious queries, and I
heartily recommend it to my fellow writers.

It so happens that I have quoted Max Perkins both
to my editors and publishers, not out of smugness but
in desperation. And always the provocation has been
the same: not one of my books bears the title I had
chosen for it, although I admittedly came very close the
third time around.

Waxing poetic, I decided to call my first work *The
Music of the Spheres*, after the Pythagorean vision that the
cosmos is nothing less than a grand symphony, each
planet and star perfectly attuned by harmonic regularity. My editor, a young martinet who has since exited
the stage by popular demand, not only rejected my
choice but scoffed, "It sounds like a treatise on the gears
of a merry-go-round calliope." I was forced to draw on
my list of reserves, but each entry was greeted by the
same derision. The editor soon began sending me selec-
tions of his own, and I returned his sarcasm in spades.
With the deadline for printing close at hand, I finally
received a call from my agent who broke the disheartening news. A list of three titles would soon arrive in the
mail, all of the editor's choosing. If I refused to pick
from among them, the choice would be made for me.
My only recourse was to withdraw the manuscript and
return the advance, which for a fledgling writer living
behind the cornstalk curtain could prove disastrous.
"Word of such conduct has a way of getting around," he
warned.

Two of the alternatives were abominable, while the
third, *This Wild Abyss*, was truly elegant—no surprise

considering that it was lifted from Book II of *Paradise Lost*. As Milton sets the scene, Satan is standing majestically on the brink of Hell, pondering his voyage across "the womb of Nature" and out into the great void where the "Almighty Maker" stores the dark materials with which to create more worlds. Although I knew I would have to accede, Milton's eloquence failed to stir me. After all, his was a vision of absolute chaos, of an unsettled cosmos still in the throes of gestation, of good and evil battling for the upper hand. Mine was one of order emerging from discord, of the human mind exchanging the power of prayer for the grasp of mathematical law. In return for my capitulation, the editor agreed to use my subtitle, *The Story of the Men Who Made Modern Astronomy*, and to employ Milton's passage as the introductory epigraph for the enlightenment of baffled readers.

In January 1697, Milton's contemporary, Isaac Newton, received an intriguing communication from Johann Bernoulli, mathematics professor at Basel. The letter contained two challenge problems, which no one had been able to solve. As a stalking horse for Gottfried Wilhelm Leibniz, who developed the calculus independently of Newton, Bernoulli wanted to test whether this English rival, who remained unpublished on the subject, was as knowledgeable in the new mathematics as his disciples claimed. According to Newton's niece, Catherine Barton, her uncle opened the letter late in the day, on returning home from work "very much tired." Nevertheless, Newton did not sleep until after he had solved the problems at four the next morning. Bernoulli, despite his ulterior motives, could not hide his admiration. Though Newton's solutions were published anonymously in the *Philosophical Transactions of the Royal Society*, Bernoulli knew exactly to whom the credit belonged: "I can tell the lion by the mark of his claw."

What a wonderful title for my biography: *Mark of the Lion: Isaac Newton and His Times*. In addition to describing his magnificent intellectual powers, had I not portrayed Newton as possessing the imperious gaze of the king of beasts, his countenance highlighted by a great leonine mane of glistening silver?

All was going well, at least from outward appearances. The manuscript sailed through copyediting, two book clubs agreed to market the work, and I was congratulating myself on a *fait accompli* when, like a letter from Bernoulli, the phone rang late one afternoon, cutting short my reverie. The voice on the other end was that of my editor, who seemed unusually solicitous about my health and current activities. Knowing full well where I stood on the matter of chapter titles and epigraphs, she finally summoned up her courage and came to the point. "The title of your book came in for a lot of criticism at this afternoon's sales meeting. Virtually everyone thinks it will puzzle the booksellers and cut down on the number of prepublication orders. Do you have any others in mind?"

My breathing suddenly became labored, as if a relative or close friend had died unexpectedly. "Since when did company salesmen gain the right to veto titles?" I demanded. And no, I do not have any alternatives in mind. "So far as I am concerned, this is it!"

I knew better, of course, and a week later—déjà vu. This time the manner was more conciliatory, but the message was the same. The publisher had control over this matter and *Mark of the Lion* was out. Another editor had "taken the trouble" to peruse the manuscript and was struck by one phrase in particular. How about *In the Presence of the Creator: Isaac Newton and His Times*? At least the wording was mine, along with the subtitle, but what possible marketing advantage it might have over the original escaped me; nor was my editor able to explain. I agreed, nevertheless, although something in the back of my mind made me uneasy.

It was not until almost a year later, with the arrival of the first royalty statement, that I realized what that something was. Instead of crediting me with sales for *In the Presence of the Creator*, my agent inadvertently substituted *Present at the Creation*, the title of the Pulitzer Prize-winning memoir by the late Secretary of State, Dean Acheson. Some six years later, I am still receiving semi-annual statements and modest royalty checks under that misnomer.

While researching my biography of Eiseley, I was struck by his lifelong love for the fox and its metaphorical associations. As a young man in his twenties, he had written a poem titled "Fox Curse" for the journal *Voices*:

> *Though I meekly pass*
> *Where you plow and fire,*
> *Everywhere I leave*
> *Fox fur on the wire—*
>
> *And a fox's face,*
> *Masked in human skin,*
> *Sometimes wild and sharp,*
> *Holds its laughter in.*[10]

As the poem suggests, Eiseley thought of himself as a changeling, a wild animal disguised as a man. He later employed this metaphor in correspondence with those whose curiosity about his personal life made him uncomfortable: "I have become my own 'fox at the wood's edge,' looking out at humanity with curiosity, but always ready to vanish into a bush when the hunt comes in my direction."[11] This time my title, *Fox at the Wood's Edge*, stuck, although the subtitle, *A Life of Loren Eiseley*, was changed without notice to *A Biography of Loren Eiseley*. I

nearly reached for the telephone but reconsidered on
the grounds that the third time was almost a charm. As
I write the final sentences of this essay, I do not know
who its publisher will be. Neither have I settled on a title
for this volume. When the time comes, however, I dream
of receiving a letter of the type which rendered superfluous Hemingway's thirty alternatives. "As to the title,"
Max Perkins wrote him on April 24, 1940, "I don't
believe you can possibly improve it, and I almost hope
you won't try."[12]

11

Tom, Dick, Harry, and I

If confession is good for the soul, as my elders often reminded me while I was growing up, I should have unburdened myself long ago. For, you see, I spent much of my "scandalous" adolescence in the company of a nefarious trio—or so it was alleged by my father more times than I can remember. Whenever I came in late on a Saturday night, he let me know about it at breakfast the following morning. Feigning nonchalance while reaching for the toast, he would suddenly look me squarely in the eye and exclaim, "Spent half the night chasing all over town with every Tom, Dick, and Harry, I'll bet!"

"Actually," I was tempted to reply, "I was with Dave, Jack, and John." However, after calculating the cost of such a riposte, I kept my own counsel. Lord, how I hated Sunday mornings!

I was reminded of these choleric episodes not long ago when the manuscript of the Eiseley biography was returned by the copyeditor, a nameless free lance hired by my publisher. Although I abhorred her green pencil (the handwriting appeared to be that of a woman, a judgment later confirmed by my editor), things were not going badly until I reached chapter ten, which begins with Eiseley, now thirty years of age and a newly minted Ph.D., taking his first full-time job as an assistant professor at the University of Kansas. My subject had reached his manhood at last, and "Loren" faded into the wings, having yielded his Christian name to that of his paternal forebears.

Unfortunately, the copyeditor had missed the point entirely. "In order to remain consistent," she wrote on one of her innumerable tag notes, "I have changed every reference back to Loren from Eiseley. OK?"

Not OK! My wife, who happened to be in the basement two floors below, came running when she heard my cry of anguish, which, since we are talking about confessions, was generously garnished with sprigs of nonparlor language. The many hours required to erase the hundreds of "green Lorens" from the final ten chapters did nothing to improve my humor. What was worse, the copyeditor had also taken the liberty of changing every reference in the footnotes and acknowledgements from Eiseley to Loren. I could almost hear the reviewers sniggering.

The letter to my editor that accompanied the returned manuscript read, in part:

> I am very displeased about the use of Eiseley's Christian name throughout. The copyeditor made this change without any consultation with me. I switched to his surname after Eiseley's graduation from Penn, but she failed to notice. This is a common practice among biographers when adulthood is attained. Otherwise you imply a familiarity which I . . . dislike; the subject is not, after all, my friend. . . . I changed the name back to Eiseley from chapter 10 on. Do not allow the production staff to tinker with this.

Never was righteous indignation more swiftly rewarded, not once but thrice. In the very next issue of *The New Yorker* critic Brendan Gill jumped all over Paul R. Baker, the biographer of the infamous architect Sanford White, for, among other things, Baker's inconsistency when referring to White by name:

Throughout the book, Baker, seeking to avoid the harmless duplication of his subject's surname, goes, with the tiresome regularity of a tic, from 'White' to 'Stan' and from 'Stan' to 'Stanny.' He dares to practice an even more unwelcome colloquial heartiness with the august [Charles] McKim [White's partner], who often appears as 'Charley.' Serious readers are also likely to feel that *Stanny: The Gilded Life of Stanford White* is a patronizing title; obviously intended to catch the eye of people seeking a 'good read,' it diminishes both the big, bluff, open lovable man of superb talent and the predatory, prematurely aging, and, at the time of his murder, perhaps already dying satyr.[1]

That same month, writing in *The New York Times Book Review*, one James D. Bloom called the author of *Hemingway: The Paris Years* to account for "his irritating vacillation between affectionately calling his subject Ernest and dispassionately calling him Hemingway."[2] A few pages later, in an otherwise favorable review of *Genet*, a biography of the pseudonymous expatriate writer Janet Flanner, author Brenda Wineapple received the following rebuke. "The author's use of first names is an annoying, not a very dignified approach to a dignified woman. When more than a few women are discussed, the book reads like a bridge party invitation list. There's Gertrude and Alice, Janet, Noel, Nancy, Solita and so on."[3]

Although I cannot be certain, I suspect that Wineapple had simply done what comes naturally, which is to say culturally. Women writers, most reviewers included, have been more reticent than men to employ last names, perhaps because theirs traditionally changed with marriage. And even when they do, women add such qualifiers as Mr. or Ms. No doubt I had been too hard on my copyeditor, who sincerely felt that she was acting in my best interests.

Males, on the other hand, grow comfortable with

their surnames at an early age; like the author of
Hemingway, they often use first and last names inter-
changeably, drawing no distinction between strangers
and friends.

This is not to say that the method of naming I
adopted after reading scores of biographies is foolproof. Whether or not the reader takes note, few things
wear more heavily on the author than the infinite repe-
tition of the same name—line after line, paragraph after
paragraph, page after endless page. It sticks in the
throat, blurs the vision, eats at the prose like an insidi-
ous tumor. The longer the surname, the worse it becomes; Valhalla must have a special sanctuary for the
souls of those who write the lives of a Rimsky-Korsakov,
a Mies van der Rohe, a Chateaubriand, or a Marquise
de Pompadour.

To alleviate this condition, certain biographers, such
as Justin Kaplan, have become masters of the pronoun.
The names Twain, Steffens, or Whitman may appear
only once or twice a page, the rest being left to the
clever use of the unobtrusive "he." I have emulated
Kaplan more than once, but rarely with success. The
copyeditor inevitably calls me to account, arguing that
the name of my subject must *always* appear at the
beginning of a new paragraph, no matter how obvious
the connection to the previous one. That is the rule;
presumably it will not change until such time as I either
write a best-seller or drop dead, and there seems little
doubt as to which will come first.

There are also times when the distance between my
subject and myself narrows considerably, despite the
disclaimer to my editor. Eiseley fell in love with Mabel
Langdon while he was still Loren in the early chapters
of the manuscript. Forever after, when discussing the
couple in their domestic setting, I found it exceedingly
difficult to write of Mabel and Eiseley, as if he were a

stranger to the woman he lived with for almost forty years. The same was true when certain friends of his youth, who also became mine during the interview process, reappeared as aging men and women in the final chapters. How stilted, I thought, to write of Emery, Bert, Marian, Rudolph, and Eiseley. By their very nature, reunions are emotional occasions; like bridge parties, they demand first names, and I occasionally used them.

I also found that the more I learned about Eiseley the more his Christian named seemed to suit. To me, at least, Loren is suggestive of stolidity, of inertia, of what the grown-ups in my family used to call "an old shoe." Moreover, he was "a chip off the old block," fathered by a well-meaning but less than ambitious traveling salesman named Clyde.

So far as I can remember, aside from repetitiveness no such problems cropped up while I was writing the life of Isaac Newton. His given name did not last beyond the first chapter. This, of course, is partly due to the fact that Newton is now more than two and one-half centuries removed from us. Familiarity does not come easily when one is writing a life lived in Restoration England. Nor did Newton have a wife and family to soften the hard edges with which he fractured many a rival's heart. And he was hardly familiar with his contemporaries, among whom he had no peers. Still, the deeper answer would seem to lie elsewhere. Einstein, the gentle pacifist, is of our time, yet no biographer that I am aware of has dared refer to him as Albert beyond his adolescent years. After he escaped Nazi Germany, Neils Bohr was the only man who took the liberty of using Einstein's given name. Besides, the very thought borders on sacrilege. Gravitation and relativity, the majestic laws that govern our universe, have no Christian names, and neither do the human gods who formulated them.

Yet the history of science is not without its exceptions, a thought that dawned on me as I was writing short biographies of the great astronomers several years ago. Tycho Brahe, history's most accomplished naked eye observer, is written of and indexed by his first name as often as not. And rarely is the more famous Galileo ever so much as mentioned by his venerable Tuscan surname, Galilei, which most laymen would undoubtedly consider a misprint. Just why this is so is difficult to say, but it probably has something to do with personality and temperament. Both men were arrogant, witty, brash, iconoclastic and, to those privileged enough to be admitted to their inner circle, wholly endearing. A charmed Cardinal Maffeo Barberini wrote Galileo a letter warmly praising the astronomer's *Letters on Sunspots*, this notwithstanding the work's open advocacy of the Copernican system. Seven years later, in 1620, in spite of growing clerical opposition to the new astronomy, Barberini presented Galileo with a poem of his own creation titled *Adulatio Perniciosa* (*Dangerous Adulation*). It was only after he donned the shoes of the fisherman as Pope Urban VIII that Barberini, who had the birds living in the Vatican gardens poisoned because they disturbed his thinking, turned on his clever friend, bringing him literally to his knees.

Along with Tom, Dick and Harry, the biographer himself is persona non grata, at least insofar as the contents of his own work are concerned. Would-be historians are taught from the outset that the first person "I" must be avoided at all costs, what Edward Gibbon once denounced as "the most disgusting of pronouns." In the words of the late John Clive, "The reasons lie partly in modesty, partly in the assumption that the ever-beckoning, though illusory, goal of 'objectivity' is somehow fostered by an impersonal mode of writing—perhaps mainly in the conviction that good taste dictates distance between author and reader."[4]

Nevertheless, Gibbon, as well as Macaulay, Carlyle, Parkman and other nineteenth-century lions, occasionally violated chastity by dropping the editorial "we" or stepping out from behind the disguise of "the historian" or "the writer." Macaulay began his masterwork in the first person: "I propose to write the history of England from the accession of King James the Second down to a time which is within the memory of men still living."[5] Gibbon ended his on an equally personal, if more melancholy, note: "It was among the ruins of the Capitol that I first conceived the idea of a work which has amused and exercised near twenty years of my life, and which, however inadequate to my own wishes, I finally deliver to the curiosity and candor of the public."[6] In between, modest sprinklings of "I" and "my" add leaven to the loaf, a subtle reminder to their readers that the writing of history is, after all, a human enterprise, and an artistic one at that.

Having begun this piece with a confession, I may as well end it with another. Only rarely have I thought twice about urging my students not to employ "that most disgusting of pronouns" in their writing. Yet how liberating it has been, while composing this group of essays, to invoke the first person, as I have never been free to do before. So here's to you, Tom, Dick and Harry! You may have made my adolescence miserable, but you are a refreshing exception to Copernicus and Kepler and Newton and Eiseley and every other surname that has plagued my writing since graduate school. I salute you one and all, wherever you may be!

12

Rendezvous in Hell

It is late of a mid-winter afternoon when my wife and I cross the bridge spanning a turgid Wabash River and enter Illinois. We turn northward, headed for my in-laws, with whom we will spend part of the holiday season. The monotonous leaden sky blends with the monotonous leaden highway, both of which stretch to inifinity in the gloaming. As always, the long drive in the silent automobile transforms us into philosophers: we soon part company and withdraw into the private confines of inner space.

On the edge of a plowed field stands a young cock pheasant, looking for all the world like the last of his species. He alone remains where, less than a generation past, scores sometimes hundreds, of ringnecks gathered to feed and crow at dusk. A sentiment captured by the naturalist Aldo Leopold comes to mind: Country becomes land when wildlife ceases to exist. Unlike the vanishing game birds, who leave no trace of their eviction, the remnants of a once flourishing civilization stand out in melancholy relief. From amid a tangle of vines and scrub and litter emerges the outline of a large frame house, windows cracked and broken, paint scaling, shingles splintered and moldering. A great weathered barn, the last of the outbuildings, is canted at an odd angle, defying gravity as much out of habit as any principle known to science. In the side yard is a forlorn rhododendron planted in some forgotten spring by a couple who dreamed wistfully of blossoms for all the springs to come; on the sagging porch sits an abandoned washboard, its corrugations almost worn through with the ritual cleansings of a thousand Mondays. At some point the harvests had failed to keep up with the bank payments and the auctioneer's gavel signaled the end. The current once supplied by the REA was shut off, the telephone, on which one could eavesdrop on one's equally lonely neighbors, disconnected. The inhabitants drove down the lane and out the gate for the last time, leaving nature and the seasons to do their duty.

This scene repeats itself many times before we reach our destination. With each reprise, my mind automatically retreats into Proust's *temps perdu*.

Did they really have to go? I keep asking myself, knowing full well that I am a witness to the end of hope. The thought occurs to me that I might buy such a place, put a light in the window, refurbish it room by room, prop up the old barn, get a horse—maybe even a goat— and write to my heart's content, far removed from the city with its noise and mindless wastage of resources. A pipe dream to be sure. Common sense informs me that the pangs of loneliness and boredom would set in about the time I was writing out the check for the first mortgage payment.

Truth to tell, it is the lives of those who once occupied these derelict precincts that interest me—the nameless inhabitants of the farmhouse who twice each day for fifty years disappeared into the barn at milking time; the all-night vigils during calving; the endless race with insects and foul weather for a living share of the harvest; the Christmas of the great snow; the print dresses and aprons crafted from carefully chosen sacks of chicken feed; the egg money that went for a daughter's class ring; the oldest son who, unable to look his father in the face, said, "No, there has to be a better way," and left after high school graduation to settle in some distant town.

As he contemplates such sacrifice and rejection, it dawns on the driver that he is feeling sorry for himself. After years of laboring in isolation his latest work is about to be released into a harsh and unforgiving world, and he wishes that, at least for the moment, he were anything but a writer. He suddenly becomes envious of the artist, who, in the time it takes the biographer to survey a single life, may turn out a hundred canvases or a thousand water colors, destroy those he doesn't care for, and still have enough to fill a small gallery. So too are the composer, the potter, the choreographer, the sculptor able to apportion risk among multiple creations. But like the groundhog in search of his shadow, the biographer briefly pokes his head above the earth, suffers the equivalent of the Chinese water torture— otherwise known as the drip, drip, drip of book reviews—then retreats into the obscurity of his burrow to pass another four or five years before warily venturing forth again.

Publication jitters are natural, of course, but what most readers and many aspiring writers do not realize is that the review process begins long before a book is finished, indeed often before the first sentence of the first chapter is ever written.

I was in Philadelphia, doing research in August 1984, when I mailed the proposal for my biography of Loren Eiseley to my literary agent in New York. Photocopies of our correspondence indicate that I was in unusually high spirits. "I am informed by my editor that she has just received a UPI review of the Newton biography which will be syndicated, but I do not yet have a copy. She said it is excellent." Thanks to the announcement of a summer research stipend awarded me by the American Council of Learned Societies, several university presses and one or two small but respected commercial publishers had recently approached me concerning Eiseley. I drafted polite but noncommittal letters to each and suggested to my agent that he first approach the five or so publishers with whom my subject was most closely associated.

His reply reached me within a week:

> While I believe selling a biography of Eiseley will be somewhat more difficult than your Sir Isaac Newton work, I'd be willing to give it a try. However, I think the outline in its present form is too dry to show to the type of trade houses you mentioned in your letter. . . . Remember that even while a number of publishers have been associated with Eiseley, editors who may be making a decision about your biography may not be well acquainted with him and his background.

Although time would prove him right, he had unwittingly loosed that old demon self-doubt, compelling me to defend a somewhat bruised ego. "I am aware that many authors look upon their work as the greatest thing since ice cream, particularly their latest brain child. I share this weakness, although I try to temper my enthusiasm." I went on to point out that Eiseley had been read by millions and had worked with editors and publishers whose names read like a *Who's Who* in the literary world: Cass Canfield, Sr., Bennett Cerf, Charles Scribner, Jr., Hiram Haydn, and Jason Epstein, among others. Finally, my Midwestern upbringing had nurtured a strong aversion to drumbeating on my own behalf: "I find it hard to envision writing the type of promotional document you have in mind. I thought what I sent along spoke for me, and rather well." Yet in the end, I knew of only one way to handle my agent's disconcerting response. "Labor Day and I have not lived up to its ideals," I wrote in early September, "for I have worked through the entire three-day weekend. Enclosed is the product of my efforts [an 18-page prospectus] which, I sincerely hope, you will find to your liking."

My agent seemed satisfied, and I gladly returned to my research while he circulated the prospectus among New York's publishing elite. The first reply, drafted by no less than a vice president, came three weeks later: "The biography of Loren Eiseley should make a nice book, but I doubt we could sell enough copies to break even. He was a fine writer, but his life does not seem especially dramatic. Good luck with it." The then president and publisher of another top firm checked in a few days later with virtually the same assessment: "I'm afraid I'm going to pass on this Eiseley biographer. The author has good credentials and undoubtedly will do a good job, but I just can't persuade myself that we can do much with this subject." When a mere senior editor subsequently responded in the same vein I began to suspect a conspiracy, or at the very least that someone was reading my agent's mail: "This is a solid idea, and Christianson appears to be a good writer, but I suspect it will generate more prestige than sales, at least for us." Another vice president, obviously a co-conspirator with an uneasy conscience, wrote not only to my agent but to me: "Well, by now you know that we've not made an offer to publish your biography of Loren Eiseley. But it's not because I didn't like the proposal; I liked it a lot, as did a couple of other readers. We all ran up against the same problem and that is a healthy fear of low sales on the part of our own sales staff and a couple of other influential colleagues." He closed with an expression of hope that we might be able to work together on some

other project in the future. "I know the Eiseley book
will be well-received."

"Only," I shot back in my mind, "if I borrow on the
equity in my home and publish with a vanity press."

Even though six years have passed and the Eiseley
biography has since been judged something of a commercial and artistic success, I can feel the hollow in my
stomach expand as, one by one, I ponder these bittersweet missives, the most wrenching of which was drafted
by an editor on the distaff side.

> I was immediately impressed with the outline and pro-
> posal for the biography of Loren Eiseley. In form and
> approach, by the way, this proposal is about as good as
> any I've seen: you want to keep it as a sample to show to
> writing students and aspiring geniuses who attend pub-
> lishing symposiums and want to know how to persuade
> publishers to buy their wares. Professor Christianson is
> obviously a very good writer indeed, and beautifully
> suited to his subject.

Surely, I remember thinking, there is no turning back
now; this most discerning lady is going to publish my
wares! On the book's spine will appear the imprint of a
long ship rigged with a single square sail, the same
vessel that once bore my Norse ancestors across a forbidding North Atlantic. But as I read on it became apparent
that the sea was running full against me:

> My difficulty is that I don't think his subject is very
> compelling! It is one thing to deploy these extraordinary
> biographical talents upon somebody of the stature of
> Isaac Newton, and I'm jealous of the publisher who had
> the good fortune to publish *that* book, but I honestly
> don't think there's much of a market for a biography of
> Loren Eiseley, beloved as his writing may be. . . . I may be
> quite wrong, but somehow I feel that this is not an ideal
> deployment of Professor Christianson's talents, no matter
> how worthy and respectable the idea is.

This argument was not new to me, and I was relieved that my wife had not been present to share this disheartening assessment, with which she would have readily agreed. Nor would it have done any good to dispute certain of the editor's other claims. As a matter of fact, the manuscript of Newton had been submitted to her firm, which declined to make an offer on the grounds that it was not commercially viable.

The rejections continued to trickle in, each a virtual clone of the last. The praise for my literary skills, which would have had me dancing a jig earlier on in my writing career, seemed suspiciously disingenuous: "The book won't sell, but we know it will be a great book."

Ironically, the research was going even better than I had expected, convincing me once and for all that a fine biography lay hidden somewhere among those thousands of pages of documents. In an attempt to bring my roller-coaster hopes under control, I telephoned New York and told my agent to contact me only if the news underwent a major change for the better. Meanwhile, I took some solace in the queries from the university presses and thanked my stars for having the sense to keep on their good side. There was also an offer from the publisher of my first two books, but I had promised myself to look elsewhere, Newton having just gone into a fourth printing, a fact barely acknowledged during contract negotiations. I thought wistfully of my early writing days, when, with a confidence (or was it naiveté?) and single-mindedness that shock me now, I completed a 600-page manuscript before thinking seriously about who, if anyone, might be willing to publish it.

Six months later, well after my return to the classroom and the blank page, a long-awaited Manila envelope arrived from my agent. "I'm pleased to send you herewith three copies, finally, of the contracts with Henry Holt for your biography of Loren Eiseley (which, although the contract manager told me he's a great fan of Eiseley, he managed to misspell on the contract)."

"That third 'e' gets em every time," I joked in my cover letter accompanying the signed documents. The only sticking point in the negotiations had been the old bugaboo, sales appeal. The editor-in-chief had insisted on speaking directly to me about my thoughts on the matter. For a second time I overcame my reticence to crow like a pet rooster and assured him that Eiseley's publishing record alone (an estimated two million volumes) should stand us in good stead in the market place. The guarded voice on the other end of the line seemed a bit weary, so I launched into a soothing monologue on my subject's multiple and unique virtues as a twentieth-century man of letters. Although I believed what I said, and still do, I learned long ago from observing my father that, more than the rest of us, salesmen love to be sold; a pregnant sigh or two reassured me that this was still so.

Despite frequent disclaimers, few writers are disinterested in the fate of their work once it appears between covers. As proof of this assertion, I direct the reader's attention to those frequently overlooked sections of a book titled Preface and Acknowledgements. If the author is married, his or her spouse is almost always cited with gratitude as the first reviewer. There then follows a list of friends and colleagues who have helped see the author through his ordeal by reading the manuscript, a ticklish proposition at best. Yet even this is not always deemed sufficient. Many writers, especially academics, farm out their work chapter by chapter, entrusting this expert or that only with those pages which fall within their purview—the theory being that greater accuracy will result. Nor, it is hoped, will this not so subliminal message be lost on future reviewers, especially when the manuscript readers have what is commonly known as "name recognition."

There is an added motive behind this exercise, one often unknown to the reader but paramount in the author's thinking. Editors at every academic press, and many commercial houses as well, are required to consult one or more outside experts before agreeing to publish a manuscript. Such reviews are not only time-consuming and costly, but often demeaning to the author, if not downright maddening. For while the author's identity is usually known to the reviewer, the reviewer is protected by a cloak of anonymity. Contrary to a court of law, one never has the opportunity to challenge the prosecution's witness directly; most important of all, the author is usually presumed "guilty" and may never be given the chance to contradict negative testimony. Thus he attempts to outmaneuver both editor and manuscript reader beforehand by trotting out his own expert witnesses, sometimes successfully, sometimes not.

I am reminded in this regard of a colleague who has three books to his credit and is soon to publish a fourth. He is nothing if not a consummate scholar and a fine writer as well. Yet he recently found himself enmeshed in the very trap described above. What makes his case even more compelling is the fact that the paid reader, after drafting six single-spaced pages of criticism, concluded by recommending publication, but devoted only a short paragraph to his imprimatur. After temporizing several months, the skittish editor finally returned my colleague's battered manuscript with regrets. More months passed before a wiser hand at another press took it on, delaying research on another book by almost two years.

The advantage to the author of having a signed contract before his book is completed becomes clear at this juncture, especially if he has also obtained an advance with which to sustain the research and writing. Although the finished product may yet be rejected, the author is likely to receive a more sympathetic hearing than my unfortunate friend and, if all else fails, walk away with a not quite so empty pocket.

This is not to say that the use of manuscript readers is a wholly futile undertaking, but many such scholars know both too much and too little about the subject in question. They feel they must say something bordering on the profound, and at great length, if only to prove themselves worthy of being called upon again. Moreover, any number of readers, like any number of book reviewers, will inevitably come up with widely divergent assessments of a manuscript. Only when the same criticisms resurface should one begin to worry. It is the editor's responsibility to differentiate between taste and questionable scholarship, and to have at least as much confidence in the person who has written a manuscript as the one reviewing it anonymously for profit.

Aside from my own publishing experience and occasional conversations with fellow authors, my knowledge of the review process derived largely from what I had read in articles, mostly written by the aggrieved. It had never occurred to me, as I began researching the Eiseley biography, that "the man with the golden pen," as he was once described, shrank when the time came to submit a manuscript to his publisher, which partially explains why he rarely met a contractual deadline.

Having established his reputation as an essayist in *Harper's Magazine* during the mid-forties, Eiseley was persuaded by his editor Jack Fischer to compile a volume of his mostly published pieces for the parent firm of Harper and Brothers. The agreement was reached in 1948, but nothing further was heard of the book until December 1952, when the author informed Fischer that he hoped to have a first draft ready by the end of the coming summer, if not sooner. He also noted that the work had taken a "philosophical twist," causing him great difficulties in terms of its organization. With publication tentatively scheduled for early 1954, Fischer gave Eiseley another seven months to deliver the first three chapters, plus a synopsis of the remainder. By now, however, Fischer had become dubious about the author's ability to complete what he had been promising for nearly five years. The gifted essayist with a unique angle of vision seemed incapable of producing anything longer than fifteen typewritten pages. Yet Fischer was not concerned with length; rather, he wanted Eiseley to forge his published material into a coherent whole by linking one essay to the next via some transitional paragraphs. Another three years passed during which Eiseley did nothing to convince Harper's that he was any closer to reaching the publisher's objective.

Among several other editors interested in Eiseley was Hiram Haydn, a Columbia Ph.D. and the author of five novels. Haydn was editor-in-chief at Random House and had recently taken on the additional responsibility of editing *The American Scholar*, the literary quarterly of Phi Beta Kappa. When, in December 1955, Eiseley submitted his essay "The Judgment of the Birds" to the *Scholar*, Haydn almost levitated. Terming it "a marvel," the editor of William Styron, Wright Morris, William Faulkner, and Kenneth Kenniston pronounced the essay "the most beautiful piece of writing I have read in several years."[1] Seven months later Eiseley wrote Jack Fischer, who had turned down the essay for publication in *Harper's*, to inform him of his decision to switch to Random House.

In November 1956, nearly a decade after his initial discussions with Fischer, Eiseley delivered *The Immense Journey*, a slender manuscript of some 75,000 words, to the rival publisher. Feeling the need for a fresh perspective, Haydn turned the material over to fellow editor Robert Linscott for review.

To begin with, Linscott felt that certain of the chapters were repetitious and should be cut. "Essays like this—what you might call a nebulous and anthropomorphic type—read well when met one by one in magazines but too many of them together tend to be amorphous and fuzzy." He next put his finger on the very problem Fischer had never been able to resolve. "I think it would make a better book if each of the four sections had . . . something to bind them together so [it] wouldn't seem so much a collection of separate essays on a rather vague theme." Finally, Linscott singled out flaws in several of the individual pieces. "The Places Below": "I'd omit this one. . . . I'm bothered by the imprecision and vagueness. What and where is the Blue Room? All through the book I kept asking myself who, what, where, when?" "The Reaching Out": "I don't understand the incident of the 'Great Voyage.' He couldn't swim, yet he appears to have swum or floated down a river." "The Fire Apes": "The last two paragraphs are an example of how the author succumbs to the temptation of going anthropomorphic. It's cute but is it science?" Not until after midnight did Linscott write his concluding paragraph, which, in the long run, proved more telling than the rest of his observations combined: "As you see I've been much too literal, probably because, in a semi-scientific book, I anticipate more facts and fewer fancies—and passed quite over its good qualities. Disregard everything I've said; publish just as is, and you'll still have a book that quickens the imagination."[2]

Perplexed and somewhat shaken by his colleague's reaction, Haydn postponed his next meeting with the author until Robert. D. Loomis, a second editor, could review the manuscript. Loomis's critique ran to four single-spaced pages.

> Mr. Eiseley is something of a mystic, and also something of a bogie-man: rats sit on his chest at night, water-bugs run across his living room, domestic cattle stampede him, herons threaten to poke him dead, a squirrel who manages to leap and claw his way into a bread box meant only for birds signifies, to the author, the doom of mankind. In much of this I sensed a sentimentality—because these incidents are, in themselves, only out-of-the-way (and seem even moreso because they all, and more, happen to one man) and the meanings found in them are arbitrary. . . . [Each] occurence brings forth cosmic conclusions, conclusions which afterward seemed to me to be exaggerated and capable of being fitted to any number of other experiences.

Yet by the time Loomis had finished, he also realized that the manuscript was equal to something more than the sum of its parts. "I think the author's real value is in his ability to make us aware, to shake up our egotistic complacency, of the unfathomable mystery of life and the wonder of the world."[3]

Haydn, who was cognizant of Eiseley's delicately balanced psyche, gritted his teeth before handing over the reviews during an all-day session on the manuscript in the author's apartment. Whether the book would ever see the light of day had suddenly become an open question. Ironically, Haydn and Random House were having no second thoughts, but Eiseley had been traumatized. Taking pen in hand at four o'clock in the morning, he drafted the longest of his surviving letters, which included a preamble of three pages before coming to what he termed "*the* point."

> Individually I feel . . . a little befuddled that after some 25 years in this subject of evolution a house editor has to

set me to rights about 'other species of man,' or to find that certain essays labelled 'silly,' 'melodramatic,' 'ludicrous,' are precisely ones which have been repeatedly requested for anthologies by staid English professors; this, however, does not lessen my now clear conviction that when two editors in a good house want to go out and retch in the street after reading the stuff that this ought to be enough. . . . If they want a 'scientific' book in the usual sense—Fred Hoyle, John Pfeifer, etc. they know where to find these men. I even suggest they may like to see how scientific I can get when I choose to practice my profession!

He felt like the Martian boy in Ray Bradbury's story who had the power of assuming the features of whatever loved one a person had lost: "In the end the boy is drained and destroyed by the contradictory and insatiable appetites of the people with whom he associated. More and more I see in this the story of a wonderful allegory of the writer; he is denounced, loved inordinately, and finally rejected if he chooses to retain a shred of his own personality and express it in his work." What was the use of continuing? He was indebted to Haydn for showing him that essays are on one side of the fence, science "forever" on the other. For too long he had been leading a divided life, reading and writing literary material when he should have kept to the bone trade. "Though it is late, I am strongly impelled to go back."[4]

Having vented his spleen, Eiseley waited for a response from New York, which came immediately in the form of a telephone call. Haydn followed up with a soothing letter, but the dark cloud had already begun to lift by the time it arrived. Eiseley was willing to give the manuscript one more try.

The Immense Journey, Eiseley's first book, became his most popular and enduring work, yet the harm he sustained was permanent. James Hahn, his nephew, reflected that whenever one of his uncle's books was about to be released Loren literally ran for cover, holing up in the apartment for a few days until word got around that the first reviews were in hand.

For the most part Eiseley need not have worried; a good eighty percent of the critics were on his side. However, it was inevitably the negative review that claimed his undivided attention. In the scientific world, writers who possess a captivating literary style may be regarded with deep suspicion. In attempting to convey a sense of joy and wonder, they reveal, it is charged, the indelible taint of the novice. Haydn caught a whiff of this hauteur when he sent an advance copy of *The Immense Journey* to Marston Bates, hoping to obtain a quote for the dust jacket. The University of Michigan zoologist, who was known for serving his guests insect hors d'oeuvres with an anticipatory smile, replied: "Sorry, I can't think of anything neat or pointed to say."[5] Meanwhile, Eiseley was pestering his editor about an old academic rival "who reviews a great deal for the *Times*," as if Haydn could dictate who the reviewer would be.[6]

It so happened that the professional attack Eiseley had long anticipated came not on his first volume of essays but on his second, *The Firmament of Time*, a finalist for a National Book Award. John Beuttner-Janusch, a firey young professor at Yale, published a devastating review in the *American Anthropologist*, the most prestigious journal in the field. Calling himself "a mere physical anthropologist," the academic proceeded to shred the work chapter by chapter, unleashing such barbs as "sentimental," "trite," "verbal brambles," and "a series of moral parables on a somewhat higher level than those found in the repertory of a fundamentalist preacher." "As is already obvious," he wrote in mocking conclusion, "the reviewer is disappointed by this book," which is not, as it purported to be, an essay in the history of science but a "work of obscurantism. Science *is* exciting and absorbing because of what it is, and, even for undergraduates, we need not inject mystery, fevered prose, overblown metaphors, and sentimental twaddle into our subject."[7] Worse still, his review of *Man in Process* by Ashley Montagu, the unnamed rival whose censure Eiseley needlessly feared, wound up on the same page as that of *The Firmament of Time*, and was ecstatic by comparison.

To be intuitively forewarned was not to be forearmed. Eiseley immediately telephoned his Penn colleague William Krogman, who listened sympathetically, then promised to write a letter of rebuttal to the book review editor of the journal. Denouncing the critique as a "gratuitously unkind and . . . unworthy piece of work," Krogman indulged in some polemics of his own. "B-J (whom I do not know personally) seems to have missed the spirit of this book. . . . I do hope the man is never asked to review The Book of Proverbs or the Song of Solomon!"[8] When Eiseley's copy of the letter arrived, he sat down immediately and jotted a note of thanks. "You have spoken for *The Firmament of Time* as its author could not possibly have spoken. I am deeply grateful to you and so is Mabel."[9]

Although I did not know it at the time, one of the reasons Mabel Eiseley broke her long silence and agreed to be interviewed had to do with some background material I had sent in hopes of convincing her of my sincerity. Edmund Fuller, the writer and retired book review editor for *The Wall Street Journal*, had always favored Eiseley's work. When Fuller wrote a positive review of my Newton biography, I enclosed a photocopy in the packet. Mabel made a special point of singling out this achievement when we met, but I was soon to learn that there was considerably more to the story.

When *All the Strange Hours*, Eiseley's autobiography, was published in 1975, Alden Whitman wrote the review for *The New York Times*. Whitman compared the prose to a bottle of Cliquot Club ginger ale: "full of fizz and bubbles, it goes down with a tang. But let the carbonation work off, and it is very chancy stuff indeed." The critic labelled the author's teleology "a quagmire." Seeming to argue for chance and design simultaneously, Eiseley left the reader to wonder just where this eminent anthropologist stood on evolution.[10]

One might have thought the inner dome of heaven had fallen! Mabel was almost as shaken as her husband. Fortunately for them, Fuller's review also happened to appear that very day. The critic's praise was of the highest order and eventually found its way onto the cover of the paperback edition. "[Eiseley] is one of the most remarkable individual minds among us. There is no comfort in him but often a great, brooding beauty. He inhabits sometimes the landscape of King Lear."[11]

Eiseley wrote immediately to say that Fuller had literally salvaged his and Mabel's Christmas. "I'm surprised," a somewhat embarrassed Fuller replied, "[that] you would let the *Times* review loom so large, considering the solid weight of accomplishment, appreciation, and public response behind you."[12]

Whether or not Eiseley was aware of it, he was one of those charmed writers who, for lack of a more eloquent appelation, I somewhat enviously classify as benefit-of-the doubters. Having written a masterpiece early on, they are so esteemed by the critics that a putatively negative review of a subsequent work inexplicably turns positive at the end or, failing that, is transformed into a reviewer's mea culpa. Examples abound, such as the review written for *The New York Times* by Sara Maitland, the British journalist and novelist, of Annie Dillard's *The Writing Life*. One need not read beyond the first two sentences for the tip-off of what is to come. "This is a tricky review for me to write. Annie Dillard is one of my favorite contemporary authors." Translation: "At only 111 pages, I had expected this book to be a breeze, one that would further enhance the author's already considerable reputation while casting a bit of reflected glory on the reviewer." Professionalism suddenly surfaces, if only for the moment. "So how am I to say that "The Writing Life" irritates me, that I find it overwritten, self-important and, therefore, unrevealing?" But what the Lord giveth . . . "This may of course say more about me than it does about the book." Thus does the review, if, indeed, it can be so qualified, wind on, like a tedious switchback. In the end, Maitland, fearful of detracting from the author's mystique and garnering the ire of Dillard admirers, yields to the pressure: "[F]lamboyant energy and generosity are at the heart of Ms. Dillard's craft. It is not her fault that I am not really interested in how writers write, but in what they write. In real books about real things."[13] Translation: "I should never have undertaken this review because I don't care for the book, but buy it anyway, a bargain at only $15.95."

Whatever the merits of *The Writing Life*, which to me is grossly overwritten and self-important, the fact that Dillard has penetrated the high latitudes of twentieth-century literature provides me with a sense of satisfaction, for, although we have never met, I feel that I knew her before fame paid a call.

In 1973, Dillard, then twenty-eight years old and living on a creek near Hollins, Virginia, with her husband, the poet and English professor R.H.W. Dillard, was soon to have her first book published by Harper's,

which was also serializing the manuscript. It was with
trepidation that the young woman mailed Eiseley the
first installment and sheepishly asked if he would be
willing to provide a blurb for the dust jacket. "Wright
Morris was here a year ago," she added, hoping to break
the ice. "He not only spoke of you *fondly*, but was also
very good-natured at my insistence that he speak of you
constantly."[14]

One might have suspected that Eiseley's nostalgia
over his own early success with *Harper's* would have made
him a soft touch. Instead, he drafted a long reply,
gratuitously lecturing Dillard about the intricacies and
etiquette of the publishing game without even so much
as skimming her article. In any case, he was much too
busy to take on this additional burden. However, when
the editor of the *Washington Post Book World* later con-
tacted him, he accepted an invitation to review *Pilgrim
at Tinker Creek*. While he enjoyed certain of Dillard's
unusual descriptions and unique insights, he criticized
her too frequent use of slang, such as *pizzazz*. She had
also committed the unforgivable sin of attributing to
Joseph Wood Krutch an obscure incident about a para-
sitic worm that Eiseley himself had discussed in *The
Unexpected Universe*, an oversight for which Dillard later
apologized in a touching letter.[15] This was one instance,
however, where the reviewer got caught in the backfire.
According to Caroline Werkley, Eiseley's research assistant, her boss was roundly criticized for nit-picking,
especially after *Pilgrim at Tinker Creek* was awarded a
Pulitzer Prize.[16]

More nettling than the reviewer who lacks the courage of his convictions is the one who ignores his charge
and proceeds to write about whatever comes to mind,
no matter how tangential. So widespread did this practice become in the early 1980s that I protested by

cancelling my subscription to *The New York Review of Books*, in my eyes the primary agent of this abuse. The "review" that finally did it was penned by none other than Alfred Kazin, the one-time literary editor of *The New Republic* and author of a fine autobiographical trilogy. The book in question was Elisabeth Young-Bruehl's *Hannah Arendt: For Love of the World*.

Kazin was obviously given carte blanche by the editors, and, although I haven't bothered to count every word, 8,000 seems a reasonable estimate. Unbelievably, the author and her 563-page opus are discussed in all of *three* sentences, the lengthiest of which proclaims: "Her [Arendt's] theorizing and her 'imperiousness,' as Elisabeth Young-Bruehl puts in her admiring, biography, did not prevent her from becoming a femme fatale, though she would have been puzzled by the compliment."[17] The remaining 7,950-odd words are devoted to Kazin's reflections on his acquaintance with Arendt, their circle of New York intellectuals, and *his*—not Young-Bruehl's—assessment of Arendt's place in history.

What with a distinguished critic summing up the virtues of her work in less than a paragraph, the author may have thought that she had gotten off easily, but as a reader and fellow biographer I was deeply upset. Seeking to showcase his own literary skills, the reviewer apparently forgot whose book he was reviewing—the one on the printed page or the one in his head. And why, I repeatedly asked myself, were the editors of this respected publication asleep at the switch?

The main problem, of course, is that in biography, as in other forms of nonfiction, there exists no established canon of review, a fact of which I became painfully aware when, after completing graduate school, the editor of a scholarly journal asked me to try my hand. Having published nothing more than a few mediocre articles gleaned from a dissertation best forgotten, I had not the slightest idea of what it is like to spend years laboring on a book, only to face the prospect of having it flayed in a rotten review. Nor was I heartened by the ruminations of a sagacious veteran of the historical profession: "Reviewing is an exacting, time-consuming, ill-rewarded skill likely to win the reviewer more enemies than friends, rarely undertaken by senior members of the society except as a favor to a friend, as part of a brawl with an old opponent, or more frequently as a part payment of the non-economic dues they owe their profession."[18] Having, as yet, few friends and wishing to make no enemies, I tiptoed through the potential minefield by giving the book a better hearing than it deserved, glossing over the arid terrain while extolling the virtues of the rare oaisis. Vowing not to be so unprepared in the future, I spent long hours reading reviews, both ignoble and elevating, with an eye to formulating a set of uncomplicated guidelines for myself as well as my students. While hardly foolproof, they possess the utilitarian virtue of providing a place on which to stand.

In addition to favoritism or revenge, one can think of many reasons to pen a review—prestige, vanity, the prospect of publication, in a few instances the offer of money—but only one valid reason to do so. Unless one harbors a genuine interest in the subject or its author (preferably both), it is best to decline, even at the risk of having one's name go back to the bottom of the list.

Ironically, the Preface or Introduction, which comes at the beginning of a book, is written last, when the author is running on empty. Commonly devoid of the style and literary grace one seeks in the pages that follow, it is often skimmed or overlooked altogether by the reader anxious to get on with the business at hand. But the reviewer who follows suit is courting disaster, if not for himself then for the victimized author. For to an ignored Preface can often be traced that eternal lament—"He didn't review the book I wrote but the one he wished I had written."

Also surprising is the fact that many reviewers fail to consider the audience for which a book is intended. Eiseley's wrenching brush with the caustic young professor is an excellent case in point. Indeed, one must seriously question the wisdom of publishers who send works written for the educated layperson to professional journals, were, nine times out of ten, they are pilloried by scholars fearful of their colleagues' scorn if they do otherwise. A reviewer's ego may well be inflated by killing such a work dead on the spot, but I submit that the murderer is an ass.

Frequent is the review that leaves the reader no more knowledgeable about its purported subject than when he picked it up. In addition to some background on the author's credentials, the reviewer is duty bound to devote a fair amount of his alotted space to a description of the book's contents, to wit: the review should not be approached as a monologue containing but an occasional reference to the work itself. On the other hand, as is commonplace in reviews of biography and many other literary forms, no purpose is served—other than that of filling space while taking the reviewer off the hook—by simply recounting the narrative point by point. Facts alone do not make a review any more than they constitute a life.

Having more or less fulfilled these obligations, the reviewer has reached the critical point at which he should turn creative, but always with the aim of assessing the book's fundamental strengths and weaknesses. Does it supplant previous works, or do its predecessors provide a more effective treatment of the subject? What contribution, if any, does it make to existing knowledge? Does the work have legs, or it is not even worthy of the

reader's consideration in paperback? Not least, are the
author's soul and pen laced with an ounce or two of
poetry? A good biography, like fine theatre, bestows
suspense on foregone conclusions. It somehow manages
to override a reader's knowledge of how events turned
out by recapturing the tensions and ambivalence of the
lead actor while the outcome was still hanging in the
balance. Oedipus can never elude himself but we are
with him every step of the way during his struggle.

Although I wax melancholy, it must be said that I
have been treated fairly by most reviewers, which is all a
writer can ask. Never had I been subjected to the type
of withering assault that caused one author to push his
unimpressed reviewer down a rather too long flight of
stairs, and another to promise an interesting rendezvous
in Hell with the critic who claimed that it was impossible
to trash that which was already in said condition. But
the times are not yet fulfilled, and who can say what fate
awaits my next book as it makes the rounds of the
newspapers, magazines, and journals. It is this thought,
however irrational, that further darkens an already dark
afternoon—the realization that I share more of Eiseley's
vulnerabilities than I care to admit.

I loosen my grip on the steering wheel; the road
entering my body through tire, shock absorber, and
floorboard suddenly emerges into a narrow band of
brilliant sunlight, causing me to reach for a pair of dark
glasses. Hundreds of pheasants, both irridescent roost-
ers and earth-colored hens, dot the weed-covered landscape as far as the eye can see. At first I think I might
be hallucinating, but I am soon disabused of this notion
by the set of twin reactor towers emerging to our right.
A green and white sign proclaims the thousands of
acres surrounding the nuclear power plant a game
reserve: "No Hunting. No Fishing. No Trespassing." I

mentally scold myself, a supposed writer, for not being able to divine from this surrealistic landscape a metaphor for the postmodern age. That task I leave to some future Loren Eiseley.

13

Comes the Postman

I must have been about twelve when I wrote my one
and only fan letter after watching the latest edition of
"The Jackie Gleason Show." Jackie's summer replace-
ments included the famous Dorsey brothers, Tommy
and Jimmy, one of whom played the saxophone, like
myself. (Well, not exactly.) Transported by his virtuoso
rendition of "So Rare" on the alto, I spent most of the
next morning drafting a saccharine paean to the aging
bandleader. I then stole into the kitchen and slipped a
table knife out of the silverware drawer. Ensconced
beneath my bed, I gently turned my ceramic piggy bank
upside down and, with the practiced hand of a surgeon,
removed a generous amount of hard-earned change
through the narrow opening. This I taped to a piece of
cardboard and inserted in an envelope, together with
my request that Jimmy (or was it Tommy?) mail me the
sheet music of "So Rare" as soon as he had the chance.
I laid out another three cents for postage and sent the
letter off to some nebulous address in New York City. It
is now some thirty-six years later; I am still awaiting a
reply should this essay happen to be read by an heir to
the Dorsey estate with a troubled conscience.

Whether my feeling of rejection and the loss of
money hoarded from mowing the neighbor's lawn has
had anything to do with my reticence to sing the praises
of others on paper is difficult to say. Many is the time I

have read an exceptionally fine book and composed a mental letter of gratitude to its author, then never carried through. So it was just last month when I finished George F. Kennan's elegant *Sketches From A Life.* Has anyone written a more evocative description of the aging process in a single paragraph?

A man's life, I reflected, is too long a span today for the pace of change. If he lives more than half a century, his familiar world, the world of his youth, fails him like a horse dying under its rider, and he finds himself dealing with a new one which is not really his. A curious contradiction, this: that as medicine prolongs man's span of life, the headlong pace of technological change tends to deprive him, at an earlier age than was ever before the case, of the only world he understands and the only one to which he can be fully oriented. For it is only the world of one's youth, the nature of which is absorbed with that tremendous sensitivity and thirst for impression that only childhood and early youth provide—it is only this world that answers to the description. The Western world, at least, must today be populated in very great part by people like myself who have outlived their own intellectual and emotional environment, and who are old not only in the physical and emotional sense but also in relation to the time. We older people are the guests of this age, permitted to haunt its strange and somewhat terrifying halls—in a way part of its life, like the guests in a summer hotel, yet in a similar way detached from it. We sometimes talk with the hotel staff. We are listened to with interest, amusement, or boredom, depending on the relevance of our words. Occasionally, whether by officiousness or indiscretion, we get fouled up in the life of the place. But guests we remain: it is not our hotel; we do not work there; we never fully understand what goes on in the pantries and the kitchens; we shall be leaving it; the personnel who will remain is youth. And the faces of the personnel, while sometimes cheerful, sometimes competent, sometimes strong, are nevertheless terrifying to us for the things that are not written on them.[1]

Kennan's deeply sensitive prose inspired in me what I thought was a gracious acknowledgement. But soon the process of rationalization set in. What could I possibly say that would mean anything to a former ambassador to the Soviet Union who had known virtually every major international leader of this century, a brilliant diplomat who gave up the realistic dream of becoming a great novelist, yet garnered a Pulitzer Prize and National Book Award? Similar thoughts about Peter Matthiessen, Robert Hughes, Toni Morrison, John McPhee, Annie Dillard, Kurt Vonnegut, Jr., and a score of others. Letters unwritten all.

My own reluctance on this score doubtless accounts for my surprise when fan letters began trickling in after the publication of my first book. The initial missive was written by a woman from Midlothian, Virginia, who credited me with giving herself and her husband of fifty years something to talk about:

> Treatises on astronomy are my husband's literary preferences and biographies are mine. Usually I cannot begin to decipher what he is reading and he has no interest in my choice of books. My curiosity was aroused when he kept reading excerpts from *This Wild Abyss* aloud to me. I ended up reading and enjoying every page of it. [We] had some delightful discussions and it gave him an opportunity to expound on his favorite topic (being a semi-retired professor of mathematics he *can* expound!!).

I next heard from Nolensville, Tennessee; the writer was nothing if not meticulous: "I want to give you my strongest and sincerest compliments on a fine book. I refer to your work, *This Wild Abyss: The Story of the Men Who Made Modern Astronomy* (New York: The Free Press/ Macmillan, 1978), 461 pp, $12.95." He continued:

I want to take a rather unorthodox approach to 'prove' to you that I read rather closely and carefully. Note the following typographical errors (not meant to be exhaustive; I am sure there are others—although the book as a whole is in fine shape). . . .

Also, to imperfectly write and to improperly publish a book which attempts to unnervingly contain so many *split infinitives* is to shamelessly commit a grievious grammatical error and to ingloriously and aesthetically offend some of the more pedantic readers who strive always to assiduously use proper literary style! Of course, I'm putting you on a bit there, for I realize that your field of expertise does not lie in the field of split infinitives but in a more important area. And my list of 'printer's errors' was not meant to be picky, either.

Naturally I was much relieved, but the reader will understand why I did not ask my publisher to supply the gratis copy requested for review in the *Nashville Banner*.

A professor of astronomy at a well-known California university wrote to confess his ignorance of the historical background in which many of the great scientific discoveries were made. "Your book does this better than anything I've ever read before; that is why I use it as a text. I hope you and your publisher will keep the paperback edition *in print* for some time. You might be interested," he added, "in a commentary on your book that I wrote for my students; a copy is enclosed. Please do not take my differences with you seriously; they are expressed partly to encourage discussions with my students." I knew I was in trouble when the four-page, single-spaced document took exception to the first paragraph of the Preface: "The statement relating to 'the shoulders of giants' was not original with Newton, tho [sic] his use of it is certainly the most famous. Newton said this as a boast, in that it takes a giant to be able to climb onto the shoulders of a giant." Now why hadn't I thought of that? But hang on, the master of Astronomy 385 was only just warming to his task.

p. 3. The gross identity of brain size and weight should not be taken as evidence that our brains now are as good as the Cro-Magnon's. See Carl Sagan's *Dragons of Eden* if the evolution of the brain interests you.

p. 4. I suspect cave painters represented a *larger* fraction of the human population then than graffiti 'artists' now.

p. 13. Possibly they [ancient priests] did not see the stars so well, because they did not have glasses to correct their eyes. But probably persons with eye defects didn't survive as well as now.

p. 17. Meaning here not clear to me.

I would love to continue, but since we are only 1/27th of the way through the book, perhaps it is best that we move along.

For reasons I am at a loss to explain, Bethesda, Maryland, has always been good to me:

Dear Professor Christianson:

Having greatly enjoyed your excellent book *This Wild Abyss* etc., I have today acquired a copy of your recent book on Sir Isaac Newton, *In the Presence of the Creator*, which I look forward to reading. I for one have no doubt that Newton himself, were he alive today, would be actively looking for an alternative to his own theory of universal gravitation.

Nor do I have any complaints about the letter drafted by an assistant professor of electrical engineering living in Belchertown, Massachusetts. "The other day I asked my wife to stop by the library and pick up a biography of Isaac Newton, not knowing what to expect from such an apparently weighty volume. Your style is outstandingly readable and just plain clear, which is all the more impressive considering your academic background." Stanford, Connecticut, checked in a few days later: "I enjoyed reading your biography of Newton quite a bit. It was interesting, and somewhat of a relief, to discover him as more of an extreme eccentric than a fiend. Thanks for writing it. Here are a couple of errata for you . . ." And from Riverhead in England's county Kent: "You've probably had this pointed out already, but 34 shillings is the same as £1–14s. By the way, could we get on Christian name terms?"

To those within driving distance of Wyndmoor, Pennsylvania, I can only say, "Beware of my localized powers!" There is a retired engineer living amongst you, devoting all of his waking hours to the history of science. "This has proven to be an endless, bottomless pit paved with intense enjoyment. *In the Presence of the Creator* has helped fill in this pit."

And to the senior editor who constantly admonished me about the length of the Newton biography (623 pages), I sent a copy of the following, all the way from Sheffield, England. "Your wonderful book on Newton has splendidly satisfied a hunger in me which has gnawed for 40 years. I have only one complaint: your work is too short. Thank you, sir, for an unputdownable book."

Yet another engineer living in Albuquerque, New Mexico, wrote: "I couldn't believe how in depth your book was and how much work you must have done to compile such a fascinating and detailed account of Newton's life. P.S. Could you send me a print of Newton's first portrait for my office?" I could and I did, remembering my old disappointment when "So Rare" failed to show up in the mail.

"In a few days I will be a 'senior citizen' on the retired roster," wrote a kindly gentleman from Los Gatos, California. "I would suppose that all the writings by such a giant [as Newton] would by now be cataloged, translated into modern English, and made available to the public. If such is the case, to whom should I apply?" I wrote back to suggest, as tactfully as possible, that he might begin with the extensive bibliography in my book.

More bread (or fruit to be exact) was soon cast upon the waters. "I am in the process of reading *In the Presence of the Creator*," a Lincoln, Nebraska, physician wrote, "and find it simply excellent. Because of my interest in trees, I am writing to find out if you know the name of the apple tree in the garden where Newton saw the apple fall." That one, I must admit, had me stumped. I had never seen a reference to the variety or, for that matter, given it any thought. Nevertheless, I suggested that he write a letter of inquiry to the Royal Botanical Gardens, never expecting to hear from him again. A year later found me in Lincoln delivering a lecture on Loren Eiseley, who had grown up in the city. Following my presentation, an elderly man with white hair and a patrician demeanor approached the lectern. In his hands was a large, heavily taped box. "Here," he beamed, "is your Flower of Kent, a direct descendent of the very tree that once stood in the Newton garden at Woolsthorpe." The good doctor still writes once a year to inquire after my immigrant scion, which stands in the flower garden by the garage. As yet, I haven't had the heart to tell him that the Flower of Kent has recently been renamed the Stub of Kent, thanks to the acquisition of an English bulldog puppy with no sense of his own history.

"Would you do something to please me?" a messianic

widow from northern Michigan pleaded. "I did it once, went daily to Catholic mass. Such insights flowed from that familiarity that I could never go back to being a Protestant. I would have loved to prescribe this for Isaac Newton's aging. It is a joy now that will see me through death into the presence of the Creator. Come with us." I wrote back to say how deeply I appreciated her invitation, but explained that there are some things that even an author cannot do. "I am an observer as opposed to a theoretical thinker, or a man of faith. The universe is so much bigger than me that I can't possibly understand it. I just trust myself to it and let it go at that."

Even less prepared was I for the large Manila envelopes that began wending their way to my office following publication. A reader from Chicago sent a copy of his self-published maxims. "It is an effort at synthesizing nature and spirit, concrete and abstract experience. I hope that you can write some comments to me about the book." Not wishing to crush the ego of this budding Norman Vincent Peale, I penned a few lines of tepid praise. Little did I know that a sequel was in the offing. "Enclosed is a copy for your reading pleasure. I hope you can write some comments to me." I opened the work at random and encountered the following: "The 'dream-woman' came and went. Voluptuous, enchanting curves shaped her form. The Milky Way curved. Time curved. Infinity just was." I am on the lookout for the postman and the envelope containing volume three.

One tries to be kind, but what is one to do with unsolicited, unpublishable manuscripts that bear no relationship to one's interests or expertise? Take, for example, the clinical psychologist who, after "skimming" my account of Newton's troubled youth, became convinced that my "letter of recommendation" would transform his barely literate treatise on early childhood education into the greatest thing since John Dewey. And what is my opinion, a Maryland reader demands to know, of his enclosed paper which proves "that 99 percent of the universal mass is missing." I'd really like to figure that one out but I have two classes to teach, plus a dental appointment. Maybe tomorrow; no, make that the day after. Tomorrow is for replying to a professor from Illinois, who has confided in me his design for a paper "that would explode (I prefer Mills Peirce's verb to 'demolish') the pretty but false received view of the Zenith and the Nadir of Newtonian Physics as exemplified in N. R. Hanson's essay of that title." He concludes, "You see that I trust that you will not appropriate my brilliant plan, at least not without my consent." Not a chance professor; not a chance. Consider your secret safe with me. By the way, thank you for an unputdownable letter.

Of all the correspondence I've received, my favorite is a typed postcard from Arthur Porges, a retired mathematics teacher living in Pacific Grove, California. "To distort Johnson's famous remark, yours is indeed a book which, long as it is, I, and many others would indeed wish longer! And finally, paraphrasing Pope, Newton and Newton's work lay hid in night; Macmillan said, Let Christianson be, and all was light!" I gazed out my study window, past the giant pin oak and the red maple, past the large white house with dark blue trim across the street, into the cloudless sky. For a moment the world looked just as I had always wanted it to.

Postscript

In case you wondered, I titled the manuscript *Writing Lives Is the Devil! Essays of a Biographer at Work* before any publisher had seen it.

How did I do?

Notes and Abbreviations
of Frequently Used Sources

Abbreviations

CUA
: Columbia University Library Archives, New York, New York.

CUL
: Cambridge University Library, Additional Manuscript, Cambridge, England.

IN
: *The Correspondence of Isaac Newton.* Ed. by H. W. Turnbull, J. F. Scott, A. R. Hall, and Laura Tilling. 7 vols. Cambridge, England: Cambridge University Press, 1959–77.

Keynes MS
: Keynes Manuscript Collection, King's College Library, Cambridge, England.

NYTBR
: *The New York Times Book Review*

UPT
: University of Pennsylvania Archives, Philadelphia, Pennsylvania.

One: A Conversation with Copernicus

1. Robert Gittings, *The Nature of Biography* (Seattle: University of Washington Press, 1978), 89.
2. Alexandre Koyré, *From the Closed World to the Infinite Universe* (Baltimore: The John's Hopkins Press, 1957), 34.
3. Nicolas Copernicus, *On the Revolutions of the Heavenly Spheres*, trans. by Charles Glenn Wallis in *The Great Books of the Western World* (Chicago: University of Chicago Press, 1952), XVI, 519.
4. Ibid.
5. Richard Holmes, *Footsteps: Adventures of a Romantic Biographer* (New York: Viking, 1985), 27.
6. *The Biographer's Gift: Life Histories and Humanism*, ed. by James F. Veninga (College Station: Texas A&M University Press, 1983), 35–36.
7. Holmes, *Footsteps*, 67.
8. Ibid., 26.

9. Ibid., 66.
10. John Craig, "Isaac Newton and the Counterfeiters," *Notes and Records of the Royal Society of London*, 18 (1963), 139.
11. IN, v. 4, 307.
12. Barbara Tuchman, *Practicing History* (New York: Random House, 1981), 17.
13. Friedrich Wilhelm Nietzsche, *Ecce Homo: How One Becomes What One Is*, trans. by R. J. Hollingdale (New York: Penguin Books, 1979), 37.

Two: Isaac Newton's Hair

1. P. E. Spargo and C. A. Pounds, "Newton's 'Derangement of the Intellect': New Light on an Old Problem," *Notes and Records of the Royal Society of London*, 34, no. 1 (July, 1979), 24.
2. Ibid., 28–29.
3. Keynes MS 137.
4. Louis Trenchard More, *Isaac Newton: A Biography* (New York: Charles Scribner's Sons, 1934), 127.
5. CUL Add. MS 3996, f. 96v.
6. Keynes MS 135.
7. Keynes MS 130, f. 5v.
8. IN, v. 3, 279.
9. Ibid., 280.
10. Ibid., 281–83.
11. Ibid., 283.
12. Ibid., 284.
13. Ibid., 282.
14. Spargo and Pounds, "Newton's 'Derangement of the Intellect' ", 16–17.
15. IN, v. 3, 359–60.

Three: Wither Fatio?

1. Barbara Tuchman, "Biography as a Prism of History," *Telling Lives: The Biographer's Art*, ed. by Marc Pachter (Washington, D.C.: New Republic Books, 1979), 143–44.
2. Ibid., 146–47.
3. Marc Pachter, "The Biographer Himself: An Introduction," *Telling Lives*, 5.
4. Tuchman, "Biography as a Prism of History," 133.
5. See *The Biographer's Gift: Life Histories and Humanism*, ed. by James F. Veninga (College Station: Texas A&M University Press, 1983), 63.
6. Richard de Villamil, *Newton: The Man*, (New York: Johnson Reprint Corporation, 1972), 38.
7. Voltaire, *Letters Concerning the English Nation* (London, 1733),

116–17; Thomas Maude, *Viator, a poem: or, A Journey from London to Scarborough by the Way of York* (London, 1782), iv.
8. Roger North, *The Lives of the North*, ed. by Augustus Jessopp, 3 vols. (London: G. Bell, 1890), v. 3, 284.
9. Yahuda MS 18, f. 2v. Yahuda Manuscript Collection, Jewish National and University Library, Jerusalem.
10. IN, v. 3, 45.
11. Charles Andrew Domson, *Nicholas Fatio de Dullier and the Prophets of London: An Essay in the Historical Interpretation of Natural Philosophy and Millennial Belief in the Age of Newton* (New York: Arno Press, 1981), 32–33.
12. IN, v. 3, 230; v. 7, 392.
13. Frank E. Manuel, *A Portrait of Isaac Newton* (Cambridge, MA: Harvard University Press, 1968), 199.
14. IN, v. 3, 231; v. 7, 392.
15. IN, v. 3, 232–33; v. 7, 392.
16. IN, v. 3, 241–43.
17. Ibid., 261, 263.
18. Ibid., 391.
19. Ibid., 268–69.
20. Richard Ellmann, *Literary Biography* (Oxford: The Clarendon Press, 1971), 3, 5.
21. Leon Edel, *Writing Lives: Principia Biographica* (New York: Norton, 1984), 28–29.
22. Manuel, *A Portrait of Isaac Newton*, 195.

Four: The Biographer and the Widow

1. Mabel Eiseley to Mrs. Karl Mattern, Sept. 11, 1975, Bennett Martin Public Library, Heritage Room, Lincoln, NE.
2. E. Fred Carlisle, *Loren Eiseley: The Development of a Writer* (Urbana: University of Illinois Press, 1986), xi (emphasis C's).
3. Mabel Eiseley to Dorothy Thomas Buickerood, Sept. 22, 1980 (courtesy of D. T. B.).
4. Interview with Froelich Rainey, Aug. 2, 1984.
5. Mabel Langdon, "Twilight Musing," *Prairie Schooner*, II, no. 3 (Summer, 1928), 194.
6. Rudolph Umland to G. C., Dec. 11, 1984.
7. Loren Eiseley, *Another Kind of Autumn* (New York: Charles Scribner's Sons, 1977), 57.

Five: The Lady of the Masque

1. Loren Eiseley to Rudolph Umland, Jan. 26, 1967 (courtesy of R. U.).
2. Eiseley to Lila Wyman Graves (undated), Gale E. Christianson, *Fox at the Wood's Edge: A Biography of Loren Eiseley* (Henry Holt: New York, 1990), 80–81.

3. Interview with Mabel Eiseley, Oct. 2, 1984.

4. UPT 50, E36, Caroline E. Werkley, "Report of the Loren Eiseley Collection," rev. ed., Sept. 1978, 25. "Whiskers" is dated Nov. 27, 1923.

Six: "Old RU" and "The Gaff"

1. Rudolph Umland, "What It's Like to Die and Live Again," *Esquire*, LXXVIII (November, 1972), C86B-C86D.

2. Loren Eiseley to Martin Peterson, Feb. 27, 1976 (courtesy of M. P.).

3. Loren Eiseley, *The Mind as Nature* (New York: Harper & Row, 1962), 60.

Seven: A Shiver in the Archives

1. J. H. Hexter, "The Historian and His Society: A Sociological Inquiry—Perhaps," *The Professor and the Public: The Role of the Scholar in the Modern World*, ed. by Goldwin Smith (Detroit: Wayne State University Press, 1972), 99.

2. Ibid., 100.

3. Barbara Tuchman, *Practicing History* (New York: Random House, 1981), 78.

4. Richard de Villamil, *Newton: the Man* (New York: Johnson Reprint Corporation, 1972), 50–61.

5. David Eugene Smith, "Two Unpublished Documents of Sir Isaac Newton," *Isaac Newton: 1642–1727*, ed. by W. J. Greenstreet (London: G. Bell, 1927), 19–23.

6. CUL Add. MS 3996.

7. W. A. Churchill, *Watermarks in Paper* (Amsterdam: M. Hertzberger, 1935), 21–22, xcix.

8. Thomas Fuller, *History of the University of Cambridge published with his Church history of Britain* (London, 1644), 122.

9. Robert I. White to Loren Eiseley, Apr. 29, 1970, UPT 50, E36, Box 5, f. Kent State University.

10. Eiseley to White, May, 7, 1970, UPT.

11. White to Eiseley, May 21, 1970, UPT.

12. UPT 50, E36, Box 40.

13. Loren Eiseley to Carl Wittke, Apr. 7, 1967, UPT 50, E36, Box 1, f. W.

14. Eiseley's remarks were not recorded verbatim, but he later repeated them in a letter to anthropologist Margaret Mead. UPT 50, E36, Box 1, f. M.

15. Interview with Murphy Murray, Oct. 28, 1984.

16. *Daily Pennsylvanian*, Sept. 17, 1968, 5.

17. Interview with Froelich Rainey, Aug. 2, 1984.

18. Interview with C. Bertrand Schultz, Nov. 13, 1984.

19. Loren Eiseley to Richard M. Nixon, Apr. 7, 1969, UPT 50, E36, Box 3, f. White House.
20. *Newsweek*, May 18, 1970, 32.
21. *Philadelphia Inquirer*, July 11, 1977, 4-A.

Eight: Tools of the Trade

1. NYTBR, January 14, 1990, 11.
2. *Time*, 134, no. 20, Nov. 13, 1989, 98–99. Also see Robert Caro, "Lyndon Johnson and the Roots of Power," *Extraordinary Lives*, ed. by William Zissner (New York: Houghton Mifflin, 1986), 197–231.
3. Annie Dillard, *An American Childhood* (New York: Harper & Row, 1987), 82–83.
4. Leon Edel, *Writing Lives: Principia Biographica* (New York: Norton, 1984), 218.
5. Edward Gibbon, *Memoirs of My Life*, ed by. George A. Bonnard (London: Nelson, 1966), 134.
6. Edward Abbey, *Desert Solitaire: A Season in the Wilderness* (New York: McGraw-Hill, 1968), 240, 244.

Nine: "Writing Lives Is the Devil!"

1. *The Letters of Gustave Flaubert, 1830–1857*, ed. by Francis Steegmuller, 2 vols. (Cambridge, MA: Harvard University Press: 1980), v. 1, 151–52.
2. R. D. Rosen, "The Pen is a Heavy Oar," NYTBR, April 12, 1981, 3.
3. Susan C. Feldhake, "Twenty Ways to Cure Writer's Block," *The Writer* (November, 1981), 29–30.
4. Monica Furlong, *Merton: A Biography* (San Francisco: Harper & Row, 1980), 171.
5. Barbara Tuchman, *Practicing History* (New York: Random House, 1981), 50.
6. Leon Edel, *Writing Lives: Principia Biographica* (New York: Norton, 174.
7. Joseph Campbell, *The Power of Myth* (New York: Doubleday, 1988), 92.
8. "Edmund Halley, "Ode to Newton" in Isaac Newton, *Principia*, 2 vols. (Berkeley: University of California Press, 1974), v. 1, xv.
9. See "The Devil and Daniel Webster," in *Selected Works of Stephen Vincent Benét*, 2 vols. (New York: Farrar & Rinehart, 1942), v. 2, 32–46.
10. Keynes MS 130 (5).
11. *The Letters of Virginia Woolf*, ed. by Nigel Nicolson and Joanne Tractman, 6 vols. (New York: Harcourt Brace Jovanovich, 1980), v. 6, 245, 374.

Ten: Arrows in the Blue

1. Arthur Koestler, *The Sleepwalkers: A History of Man's Changing Vision of the Universe* (New York: Macmillan, 1959), 15.
2. Interview with Wright Morris, Aug. 14, 1984.
3. UPT 50, E36, Box 8, f. *The Immense Journey.*
4. John C. Fischer to Loren Eiseley, July 19, 1948, UPT 50, E36, Box 9, f. 6, *The Immense Journey.*
5. Eiseley to Fischer, Dec. 23, 1952, UPT 50, E36, Box 1, f. F, *The Immense Journey.*
6. Fischer to Eiseley, Dec. 29, 1952, Box 9, f. 6, *The Immense Journey.*
7. Eiseley to Hiram Haydn, Nov. 14, 1956, CUA, Random House, Box 432, f. Eiseley.
8. Eiseley to Haydn, Dec. 2, 1956, UPT 50, E36, Box 9, f. 7, *The Immense Journey.*
9. *Editor to Author: The Letters of Maxwell E. Perkins*, ed. by John Hall Wheelock (New York: Grosset & Dunlap, 1950), 122.
10. Loren Eiseley, *All the Night Wings* (New York: Times Books, 1979), 42.
11. Loren Eiseley to E. Fred Carlisle, Mar. 23, 1974 (courtesy of E. F. C.).
12. *Editor to Author*, ed. by Wheelock, 157.

Eleven: Tom, Dick, Harry, and I

1. Brendan Gill, "Seeking a Likeness," *The New Yorker* (January 29, 1990), 92.
2. NYTBR, Jan. 7, 1990, 19.
3. Ibid., 25.
4. John Clive, *Not By Fact Alone: Essays on the Writing and Reading of History* (New York: Alfred Knopf, 1989), 25.
5. Thomas Babington Macaulay, *Macaulay's History of England: From the Accession of James II*, 4 vols. (New York: Dutton, 1962), v. 1, 1.
6. Edward Gibbon, *History of the Decline and Fall of the Roman Empire*, 6 vols. (London, 1788), v. 6, 646.

Twelve: Rendezvous in Hell

1. Hiram Haydn to Loren Eiseley, Dec. 20, 1955, UPT 50, E36, Box 9, f. *The Immense Journey.*
2. R. N. Linscott to Haydn, Dec. 20, 1956, CUA, Random House, Box 432, f. Eiseley.
3. Robert D. Loomis to Haydn, Jan. 20, 1957, CUA.
4. Loren Eiseley to Haydn, Jan. 30, 1957, CUA.
5. Marston Bates to Haydn, June 24, 1957, CUA.
6. Loren Eiseley to Haydn, Mar. 25, 1957, CUL.
7. *American Anthropologist* 65 (1963), 693–94.

8. W. M. Krogman to W. C. Sturtevant, July 15, 1976, UPT 50, E36, Box 1, f. K.
9. Loren Eiseley to Krogman, July 16, 1963, UPT.
10. *The New York Times*, Dec. 18, 1975, 43.
11. *The Wall Street Journal*, Dec. 18, 1975, 16.
12. Edmund Fuller to Loren Eiseley, Dec. 29, 1975, UPT 50, E36, Box 2, f. Fuller, Edmund.
13. NYTBR, Sept. 17, 1989, 15.
14. Annie Dillard to Loren Eiseley, Aug. 3, 1973, UPT 50, E36, Box 2, f. Dillard, Annie (emphasis D's).
15. *The Washington Post Book World*, Mar. 31, 1974, 3.
16. Interview with Caroline E. Werkley, June 10, 1985.
17. *The New York Review of Books*, 29, June 24, 1982, 3.
18. J. H. Hexter, "The Historian and His Society: A Sociological Inquiry—Perhaps," *The Professor and the Public: The Role of the Scholar in the Modern World*, ed. by Goldwin Smith (Detroit: Wayne State University Press, 1972), 96.

Thirteen: Comes the Postman

1. Geroge F. Kennan, *Sketches From a Life* (New York: Pantheon, 1989), 183–84.

Suggested Reading

Aaron, Daniel, ed. *Studies in Biography.* Cambridge, MA: Harvard University Press, 1978.

Altick, Richard. *Lives and Letters: A History of Literary Biographies in England and America.* New York: Alfred A. Knopf, 1965.

Ascher, Carol; DeSalvo, Louise; Ruddick, Sara, eds. *Between Women: Biographers, Novelists, Critics, Teachers and Artists Write About Their Work on Women.* Boston: Beacon Press, 1984.

Berteaux, Daniel, ed. *Biography and Society: The Life History Approach in the Social Sciences.* Beverly Hills: Sage Publications, 1981.

Bowen, Catherine Drinker. *Adventures of a Biographer.* Boston: Little Brown, 1959.

———. *Biography: The Craft and the Calling.* Boston: Little Brown, 1968.

Bradford, Gamaliel. *American Portraits, 1875–1900.* Boston and New York: Houghton Mifflin, 1932.

Coe, Richard N. *When the Grass Was Taller: Autobiography and the Experience of Childhood.* New Haven: Yale University Press, 1984.

Clifford, James L., ed. *Biography as an Art: Selected Criticism, 1560–1960.* Oxford: Oxford University Press, 1962.

———. *From Puzzles to Portraits: Problems of a Literary Biographer.* Chapel Hill: University of North Carolina Press, 1970.

Clive, John. *Not By Fact Alone: Essays on the Writing and Reading of History.* New York: Alfred A. Knopf, 1989.

Denzin, Norman K. *Interpretive Biography.* Newbury Park: Sage, 1989.

Dillard, Annie. *An American Childhood.* New York: Harper & Row, 1987.

Edel, Leon. *Literary Biography.* Bloomintgon: Indiana University Press, 1959.

———. *Writing Lives: Principia Biographica.* New York: Norton, 1984.

Ellman, Richard, *a long the riverrun: Selected Essays.* London: Hamish Hamilton Ltd., 1988.

———. *Literary Biography.* Oxford: Clarendon Press, 1971.

Epstein, William H. *Recognizing Biography.* Philadelphia: University of Pennsylvania Press, 1987.

Freud, Sigmund. *Autobiographical Study.* Trans. by James Strachey. New York: Norton, 1925.

Friedson, Anthony M., ed. *New Directions in Biography.* Honolulu: University of Hawaii Press, 1981.

Garraty, John A. *The Nature of Biography.* New York: Alfred A. Knopf, 1957.

Gay, Peter. *Freud For Historians.* New York: Oxford University Press, 1985.

Gittings, Robert. *The Nature of Biography.* Seattle: University of Washington Press, 1978.

Homberger, Eric and Charmley, John, eds. *The Troubled Face of Biography.* New York: St. Martin's Press, 1988.

Hamilton, Ian. *Keepers of the Flame: Literary Estates and the Rise of Biography.* London: Hutchinson, 1992.

Heilbrun, Carolyn. Writing a Woman's Life. New York: Norton, 1988.

Hoberman, Ruth. *Modernizing Lives: Experiments in English Biography, 1918–1939.* Carbondale: Southern Illinois University Press, 1987.

Holmes, Richard. *Footsteps: Adventures of a Romantic Biographer.* New York: Viking, 1985.

Hook, Sidney. *The Hero in History.* Boston: Beacon Press, 1943.

Hughson, Lois. *From Biography to History: The Historical Imagination and American Fiction.* Charlottesville: University Press of Virginia, 1988.

Iles, Teresa, ed. *All Sides of the Subject: Women and Biography.* New York: Teachers College Press, 1992.

Kendall, Paul Murray. *The Art of Biography.* New York: Norton, 1965.

Light, Donald, *Becoming Psychiatrists: The Professional Transformation of Self.* New York: Norton, 1980.

Lomansk, Milton. *The Biographer's Craft: Practical Advice on Writing, Shaping and Polishing Biographical Material.* New York: Harper & Row, 1986.

Mallon, Thomas. *A Book of One's Own: People and Their Diaries,* New York: Ticknor and Fields, 1984.

Mandell, Gail Porter. *Life Into Art: Conversations With Seven Contemporary Biographers.* Fayetteville: University of Arkansas Press, 1991.

Maurois, Andre. *Aspects of Biography.* New York: D. Appleton, 1930.

Mehta, Ved. *John Is Easy to Please: Encounters With the Written and the Spoken Word.* New York: Farrar, Straus and Giroux, 1971.

Meyers, Jeffrey, ed. *The Craft of Literary Biography.* London: Macmillan, 1985.

Momigliano, Arnaldo. *The Development of Greek Biography.* Cambridge, MA: Harvard University Press, 1971.

Nadel, Ira Bruce. *Fiction, Fact, and Form.* New York: St. Martin's Press, 1984.

Novarr, David. *The Lines of Life: Theories of Biography, 1880–1970.* West Lafayette: Purdue University Press, 1986.

Pachter, Marc. ed. *Telling Lives: The Biographer's Art.* Washington, D.C.: New Republic Books, 1979.

Park, Honan. *Author's Lives: On Literary Biography and the Arts of Language.* New York: St. Martin's Press, 1990.

Parke, Catherine N. *Samuel Johnson and Biographical Thinking.* Columbia: University of Missouri Press, 1991.

The Personal Narrative Group, eds. *Interpreting Women's Lives: Feminist Theory and Personal Narratives.* Bloomington: Indiana University Press, 1989.

Reid, Benjamin Lawrence. *Necessary Lives: Biographical Reflections.* Columbia: University of Missouri Press, 1990.

Runyan, William McKinley. *Life Histories and Psychobiography: Explorations in Theory and Method.* New York: Oxford University Press, 1982.

Stadter, Philip A., ed. *Plutarch and the Historical Tradition.* London and New York: Routledge, 1992.

Strachey, Giles Lytton. *Biographical Essays*. New York: Harcourt, Brace, 1949.

————. *Eminent Victorians*. London: Chatto and Windus, 1918.

Tuchman, Barbara. *Practicing History*. New York: Alfred A. Knopf, 1981.

Veninga, James F., ed. *The Biographers' Gift: Life Histories and Humanism*. College Station: Texas A&M University Press, 1983.

Vice, Giambattista. *The Autobiography*. Trans. by Max Harold Fisch and Thomas Goddard Bergin. Ithaca: Cornell University Press, 1944.

Weinberg, Steve. *Telling the Untold Story: How Investigative Reporters Are Changing the Craft of Biography*. Columbia: University of Missouri Press, 1992.

White, Robert W. *Lives in Process: A Study in the Natural Growth of Personality*. New York: Dryden, 1952.

Whittemore, Reed. *Whole Lives: Shapers of Modern Biography*. Baltimore: Johns Hopkins University Press, 1989.

Winks, Robin, ed. *The Historian as Detective: Essays on Evidence*. New York: Harper & Row, 1968.

Winslow, Donald, J. *Life-Writing: A Glossary of Terms in Biography, Autobiography, and Related Forms*. Honolulu: University of Hawaii Press, 1980.

Zinsser, William, ed. *Extraordinary Lives: The Art and Craft of American Biography*. New York: American Heritage, 1986.

Acknowledgments

Many of the debts an author incurs along the way can never be repaid, but at least they can be acknowledged. I am particularly grateful to the following institutions and their staffs: the Bennett Martin Public Library, Lincoln, Nebraska, Cambridge University Library, Columbia University Library, King's College Library, Trinity College Library, University of Nebraska Library, the University of Pennsylvania Archives, and, not least, my own Indiana State University Library.

I wish to thank especially the following individuals for favors both large and small: Laurie Bradach, James and Dolly Hahn, Wright Morris, Froelich Rainey, Rudolph Umland, and the late Mabel Eiseley and Wilbur Gaffney. A special note of gratitude is sounded for my editor and publisher James Thorpe, III, and for production manager Kathleen Browne.

Funding was generously provided by the Faculty Research Committee of Indiana State University, inspiration by the students of my course titled Biography as History.

Finally, I wish to thank Packy and the Packydoodles—Mambo Manny, Snoote Rockne, Count Blueski, the ever beautiful Lady May, and Tina Lu.

Index